THE ROMANTIC REVOLUTION

THE
ROMANTIC
REVOLUTION

TIM BLANNING

Weidenfeld & Nicolson

LONDON

First published in Great Britain in 2010
by Weidenfeld & Nicolson

1 3 5 7 9 10 8 6 4 2

A CIP catalogue record for this book is
available from the British Library.

ISBN: 978 0 297 85900 0

Typeset by Input Data Services Ltd, Bridgwater, Somerset

Printed and bound in the UK by CPI Mackays,
Chatham, Kent

The Orion Publishing Group's policy is to use papers that are natural,
renewable and recyclable and made from wood grown in sustainable
forests. The logging and manufacturing processes are expected to
conform to environmental regulations of the country of origin.

Weidenfeld & Nicolson

Orion Publishing Group Ltd
Orion House
5 Upper Saint Martin's Lane
London, WC2H 9EA

An Hachette UK Company

www.orionbooks.co.uk

CONTENTS

ILLUSTRATIONS

List of Illustrations

Francesco Hayez, *The Refugees of Parga* (1831), Pinacoteca Civica T. Martinengo, Brescia (*AKG*)

INTRODUCTION

Between the middle of the eighteenth and the middle of the nineteenth centuries, Europe changed so rapidly and radically that one can reasonably speak of a watershed in world history. Those who lived through it were constantly using the word 'revolution' to express their awareness that they were living in exciting times, as in 'the American Revolution', 'the French Revolution' or 'the industrial revolution'. To these, historians have added several others, notably 'the agrarian revolution', 'the commercial revolution', 'the communications revolution' and 'the consumer revolution'. Contemporary astonishment at the pace and variety of change was indeed acute. In 1818, for example, the German publisher Friedrich Perthes exclaimed that 'in the three generations alive today our own age has combined what cannot be combined. No sense of continuity informs the tremendous contrast inherent in the years 1750, 1789 and 1815. To people alive now, they simply do not appear as a sequence of events'.[1] Twenty years later, the Belgian music critic François Fétis, born in 1784, wrote that during his lifetime the world had changed in more ways than during all of previous human history.[2]

It was not only the material world that was affected. Those who lived to see the world of Voltaire, Reynolds and Haydn make way for the world of Hugo, Turner and Wagner could appreciate that a great cultural revolution had also occurred. This was 'the romantic revolution', which deserves to be

I

accorded the same status as the other revolutions. If it had no starting-point as clear cut as the Declaration of Independence or the Fall of the Bastille, contemporaries were well aware that a monumental upheaval in the cultural world was under way. Even those chary of acknowledging their own affiliation had to admit that they had been affected. Delacroix, for example, wrote: 'if by romanticism one understands the free manifestation of my personal impressions, my aversion to models copied in the schools, and my loathing for academic formula, I must confess that not only am I romantic, but I was so at the age of fifteen'.[3] In just two or three generations, the rule-book of the classical past was torn up. In its place came *not* another set of rules but a radically different approach to artistic creation which has provided the aesthetic axioms of the modern world, even if a definition of romanticism has proved elusive.

In December 1923 Arthur Lovejoy, professor of philosophy at Johns Hopkins University, gave a lecture to the Annual Meeting of the Modern Language Association of America entitled 'On the Discrimination of Romanticisms'.[4] He entertained his audience by listing some of the candidates previously nominated for the title of 'father of romanticism', ranging from Plato to St Paul to Francis Bacon to the Reverend Joseph Warton to Rousseau and Kant, to name just a few. After reviewing the various types of romanticism and their manifold incongruities, he concluded wearily: 'any attempt at a *general* appraisal even of a single chronologically determinate Romanticism – still more, of "Romanticism" as a whole – is a fatuity'.[5] This was a verdict repeated with varying degrees of vehemence throughout the twentieth century. In an influential book on England, for example, Marilyn Butler used the word 'romantic' in her title but then announced on the first page that it was 'anachronistic' and would not have been recognised by the poets to whom it was applied.[6]

Equally various have been the starting-points identified. They include Piranesi's *Roman Antiquities of the Time of the Republic* of 1748 (Michel Florisoone); the Lisbon earthquake of 1755 (Kenneth Clark); Rousseau's *La Nouvelle Héloïse* of 1761 (Maurice Cranston); Herder's journey to France in 1769 (Rüdiger Safranski); Blake's *Songs of Innocence* of 1789 (Maurice Bowra); and Wilhelm Heinrich Wackenroder and Ludwig Tieck's *Heart-felt Effusions of an Art-loving Monk* of 1797 (Hans-Joachim Schoeps).[7] Other popular runners are Rousseau's conversion experience on the road to Vincennes in 1749; Horace Walpole's nightmare which led to the writing of his Gothic novel *The Castle of Otranto* in 1764; and Goethe's enthusiastic response to Strassburg Cathedral in 1770.

Much scholarly energy has also been devoted to establishing when the word 'romantic' first made an appearance. The first recorded occurrence was in the title of a quaint little book published in 1650: *Herba parietis: or, The wall-flower as it grew out of the stone chamber belonging to the metropolitan prison of London, called Newgate: being a history which is partly true, partly romantick, morally divine: whereby a marriage between reality and fancy is solemnized by divinity*. This had been written by the Catholic royalist Thomas Bayly 'whilst he was a prisoner there'.[8] Nine years later occurred the first mention thought worthy of inclusion in the *Oxford English Dictionary*, this time by the Anglican divine Henry More of Christ's College, Cambridge, when he wrote in his treatise on the *Immortality of the Soul*: 'I speak especially of that Imagination which is most free, such as we use in Romantick Inventions'.[9] It was also being used in English in the mid-seventeenth century to describe picturesque landscapes and buildings, as in Samuel Pepys' view that Windsor Castle was 'the most romantique castle that is in the world'. More usually, however, it was used in a pejorative sense, to refer disparagingly to fantastic baroque novels written 'like the old romances' and it was also in that sense that it first appeared as '*romanesque*' in the dictionary of the Académie française in 1694.[10] By the 1730s, as '*romantisch*' it had found its way into German-language periodicals.[11]

In the course of the eighteenth century it slowly began to shift towards its modern meaning. An early sign was the Poet Laureate Thomas Warton's treatise on 'The Origin of Romantic Fiction in Europe' of 1774, in which he drew a distinction between literature he called 'romantic' and the classical tradition. Dante's *Divine Comedy*, for example, he called 'a wonderful compound of classical and romantic fancy'.[12] But Warton was using the word in a descriptive and chronological sense. It was in Germany at the turn of the nineteenth century that a clear programme was articulated and called romantic. To the fore were the Schlegel brothers, Friedrich and August Wilhelm, whose mouthpiece was the periodical *Athenæum* founded in 1798. It was also there that one of the poetic masterpieces of German romanticism was first published: 'Hymns to the Night' by 'Novalis', the *nom de plume* of the Saxon noble Friedrich von Hardenberg.

This articulation coincided with a rapid dissemination of German philosophy and German literature. If the Germans of the proto-romantic 'Storm and Stress' [*Sturm und Drang*] movement of the 1770s had been inspired by English writers, especially Shakespeare, the compliment was now handsomely returned by Walter Scott (by his own admission 'German mad' in the 1790s), Henry Crabb Robinson and Samuel Taylor Coleridge, to name just three of the main transmitters.[13] In continental Europe an even more important conduit was Madame de Staël's *De l'Allemagne*, not least because she was writing in the *lingua franca* of the educated. First published in London in 1813 in French, it was translated into English almost immediately.[14] Among other things, she contrasted the literature of France – 'the most classical of all' and therefore also the most elitist – with the romanticism of the Germans, populist and popular enough to have permeated society from the Rhine to the Baltic.[15] Now the references to romanticism came thick and fast across Europe. In 1817 the *'romantiki'* in Russia were denounced by the old guard as 'literary schismatics who have surrendered with body and soul to the depraved muses of the romantic Parnassus'.[16] The first French intellectual to have called himself a 'romantic' appears to have been Stendhal when writing to a friend in 1818 that 'I am a passionate romantic, that is to say I am for Shakespeare and against Racine, for Lord Byron and against Boileau'.[17] In that same year, the Polish poet Casimir Brodzinski wrote a dissertation contrasting classicism and romanticism, while at the other end of Europe, in Spain, the same distinction began to appear in the periodical press. It was also in 1818 that Goethe wrote of Italy: 'the public is divided into two factions that stand facing each other ready for battle. And whereas we Germans when the occasion arises use the adjective romantic quite peacefully, in Milan the two expressions romanticism and classicism designate two irreconcilable sects'. In 1823 the Portuguese poet Almeida Garret referred to 'we romantics'.[18] And so on.

Not everyone was sure what it meant. Prince Pyotr Andreyevich Vyazemsky, although the most forthright of the

Russian romantics, confessed in 1824: 'Romanticism is like a phantom. Many people believe in it; there is a conviction that it exists, but where are its distinctive features, how can it be defined, how can one put one's finger on it?'.[19] One thing it emphatically was not was a style. Romanesque, Gothic, Renaissance, Mannerism, Baroque and Rococo all had clear stylistic concepts, but romanticism never developed anything similar.[20] Especially in architecture almost every conceivable style was tried – neo-Gothic, neo-classical, neo-Renaissance, neo-Egyptian, neo-baroque, neo-everything. Heinrich Hübsch actually published a pamphlet in 1828 asking pathetically, *In what style should we build?*[21] The differences between – say – the paintings of Caspar David Friedrich and Eugène Delacroix, or the poetry of Novalis and Wordsworth, or the music of Wagner and Verdi (these last two were exact contemporaries born in the same year) provide sufficient evidence of stylistic diversity. The first French historian of romanticism – F. R. de Toreinx – defined his subject as 'just that which cannot be defined', while Baudelaire wrote that 'romanticism is precisely situated neither in choice of subjects nor in exact truth but in a way of feeling'.[22]

That plenty more imprecise offerings of this kind can be found should not lead to an abandonment of the quest with a despairing shrug of the shoulders. What is needed is a willingness to enter the world of the romantics by the routes they chose themselves, however shifting the sands on which that world rests and however ethereal the atmosphere in which it has its being. By its nature, romanticism does not lend itself to precise definition, exegesis and analysis. It is through sounds and images, dreams and visions, that the gate to understanding can be opened (to employ the kind of evocative language the

6

romantics themselves liked). Words have to be used but their limitations must be recognised. As Tennyson wrote in *In Memoriam*:

> I sometimes hold it half a sin
> To put in words the grief I feel:
> For words, like Nature, half reveal
> And half conceal the Soul within.[23]

It was this 'Soul within' that formed the core of the romantics' concerns. In the seventeenth and eighteenth centuries, the scientific revolution and the Enlightenment had shifted attention away from the darkness of the human interior, a zone terrorised by fear of God, towards the sunny uplands of the world outside. It was a move from theocentricity to anthropocentricity, from an overriding concern with the far side of the grave (what the Germans call *Jenseitigkeit*) to making the best of this world (*Diesseitigkeit*), for it was now seen that 'the proper study of mankind is man' (Alexander Pope). Thanks to the discoveries of the natural scientists, it was a world that could be investigated, understood, controlled and improved.

Yet when the tide was running so strongly in favour of this secular meliorism that all the old intellectual and cultural lumber looked like being washed away, it began to turn. The pace of change in so many spheres of human activity had picked up enough speed to make a growing number of people uneasy. Moreover, the jaunty triumphalism of many enlightened rationalists suggested that this was the beginning of an ever-accelerating process that would end with all the old religious, cultural and social landmarks swept away. As one ruler after another embraced the enlightened programme, it seemed that the barbarians were not only inside the gates but in full control of the citadel. Nor could this brave new world's culture satisfy all appetites. Many laughed at Voltaire's mocking satires on stupid prejudices and many felt edified by forms of religion stripped of superstition, but there were also those who thirsted after more sustaining fare than his thin gruel. On the other hand, they did not simply wish to go back to the institutions and values of the past but looked for alternatives. It was into this transcendental vacuum that the romantics moved.

In doing so, they were initiating a new phase in the long-running dialectic between a culture of feeling and a culture of reason. The former had last been in the ascendant during the baroque era before being thrust to one side by the victory of Cartesian rationalism and French classicism.[24] The family resemblance between the baroque and romanticism is especially clear in the visual arts, in the similarities between Rubens and Delacroix, for example. But the relationship between the two cultural paradigms has always been dialectical not cyclical. The romantics were not repeating their ancestors. On the contrary, they brought about a cultural revolution comparable in its radicalism and effects with the roughly contemporary American, French and industrial revolutions. By destroying natural law and by reorienting concern from the work to the artist, they tore up the old regime's aesthetic rule-book just as thoroughly as any Jacobin tore down social institutions. In the words of Ernst Troeltsch: 'romanticism too is a revolution, a thorough and genuine revolution: a revolution against the respectability of the bourgeois temper and against a universal equalitarian ethic: a revolution, above all, against the whole of the mathematico-mechanical spirit of science in western Europe, against a conception of Natural Law which sought to blend utility with morality, against the bare abstraction of a universal and equal Humanity'.[25]

As will be argued below, it was Hegel who captured the essence of this revolution in his pithy definition of romanticism as 'absolute inwardness' [*absolute Innerlichkeit*]. It will also be argued that its prophet was Jean-Jacques Rousseau: if not the most consistent, then certainly the most influential of all the eighteenth-century thinkers. Writing in 1907, Lytton Strachey caught Rousseau's special quality very well: 'among those quick, strong, fiery people of the eighteenth century, he belonged to another world – to the new world of self-consciousness, and doubt, and hesitation, of mysterious melancholy and quiet intimate delights, of long reflexions amid the solitudes of Nature, of infinite introspections amid the solitudes of the heart'.[26] Shelley, who derided the *philosophes* as 'mere reasoners', regarded Rousseau as 'a great poet'.[27]

In what follows, no attempt has been made to write a general history of romanticism. Listing the creative artists who could be categorised as 'romantic' would consume a book much longer than this relatively slender volume. I have tried to identify the most striking characteristics of the romantic revolution and to illustrate them. The Enlightenment believed that to collect and publish all human knowledge would lead to the improvement of humanity. The romantics thought they knew better.

1

THE CRISIS OF
THE AGE OF REASON

On 28 June 1751 the first volume of the *Encyclopedia, or a systematic dictionary of the sciences, arts, and crafts* (better known in its abbreviated French form as the *Encyclopédie*), edited by Jean Le Rond D'Alembert and Denis Diderot, was published in Paris. Originally intended to be nothing more than a translation of Ephraim Chambers' *Cyclopædia* of 1728, the project soon expanded to ten volumes and kept on growing. By the time it reached completion with a two-volume index in 1780 it covered thirty-five volumes containing more than 20,000,000 words. This was much more than a reference work: it was underpinned by a mission to modernise. Once all knowledge had been assembled and its fundamental principles identified, the way would be clear for further progress. It was a process that necessarily involved casting a critical eye at existing institutions, customs and values. As Diderot put it in his article on Encyclopedia: 'all things must be examined, debated, investigated without exception and without regard for anyone's feelings ... We must ride roughshod over all these ancient puerilities, overturn the barriers that reason never erected, and give back to the arts and the sciences the liberty that is so precious to them'.[1] Although the sharp eye of the censor compelled discretion, chief among those 'ancient puerilities' that Diderot had his eye on was the Catholic Church.

The impact of the *Encyclopédie* was immediate and lasting. An instant best-seller right across Europe, its sales had exceeded 25,000 complete sets by 1789, more than half of them outside France.[2] Anyone who contributed to it automatically became a celebrity: 'in the past', wrote Voltaire, 'men of letters were not admitted into polite society, they have now become a necessary part of it'.[3] Fierce opposition from the conservative press and intermittent persecution by the authorities, culminating in an outright ban by both King and Pope in 1759, helped to promote a sense of solidarity among both contributors and sympathisers, so that *'encyclopédiste'* entered the language to denote a progressive intellectual. But by the time they were forced underground, Diderot and D'Alembert had succeeded in their mission of creating an institutional centre for their project of Enlightenment.[4] Also in 1759 D'Alembert claimed in his treatise *Elements of Philosophy* : 'a most remarkable change has taken place in our ideas, a change which by its rapidity, seems to promise us a greater one yet ... Our century has called itself supremely *the century of philosophy*'.[5]

This triumphalism derived in part from the knowledge that the *Encyclopédie* was only one of many major works of enlightened philosophy to have been published around the middle of the century, including Montesquieu's *The Spirit of the Laws* in 1748, the first volume of Buffon's *Natural History* in 1749, Condillac's *Treatise on Systems*, also in 1749, and Voltaire's *The Age of Louis XIV* in 1751. Yet at the very moment that the tide seemed to be running irresistibly in their favour, a mighty splash announced the appearance of an intrepid opponent determined to swim against the current. This was Jean-Jacques Rousseau, who in July 1749 had a conversion experience while on his way to see his friend Diderot in prison at Vincennes, just outside Paris. Unable to afford a carriage, Rousseau went on foot, whiling away the time by reading the *Mercure de France*. His eye was struck by an advertisement for a prize essay competition staged by the Academy of Dijon. The topic was: 'Has the progress of the sciences and arts done more to corrupt morals or improve them?' In his autobiography *Confessions*, published posthumously in 1782, Rousseau recalled: 'The moment I read this I beheld another universe and became another man'.[6] In another account he went into more detail about the extreme nature of his reaction: 'I felt my mind dazzled by a thousand lights ... I felt my head seized by a dizziness that resembled intoxication'. Slumping to the ground, he spent the next hour in a kind of trance, sobbing so passionately that when he came to his senses he found his coat drenched with tears.[7]

The reason for this effusion was Rousseau's sudden insight that the Dijon Academy's question was not rhetorical. Collecting his wits, he set about articulating his epiphany in *A Discourse on the Moral Effects of the Arts and Sciences*, which won the prize and was published the following year. With all the zeal of the convert, he proclaimed that, contrary to expectation, the civilising process was not leading to liberation but to enslavement, as it has flung 'garlands of flowers over the chains which weigh us down', so that 'our minds have been corrupted in proportion as the arts and sciences have improved'. All the various branches of the natural sciences, he observed, have their origins in a vice: astronomy in superstition, mathematics in greed, mechanics in ambition, physics in idle curiosity. Even printing had proved to be a false friend, for it had allowed the dissemination of impious tracts, such as those of Hobbes and Spinoza. Rousseau ended his diatribe with the prediction that eventually men would become so alienated from the modern world that they would beg God to give them back their 'ignorance, innocence, and poverty, the only goods that can make for our happiness and that are precious in your sight'.[8]

This was to turn the agenda of the Enlightenment on its head with a vengeance. Throwing caution to the winds, Rousseau went out of his way to distance himself from his former friends, accusing them of subverting the traditional values of patriotism and religion in pursuit of 'the destruction and degradation of everything sacred among men'. It took a long time for the *philosophes* to realise just how extreme was Rousseau's apostasy. They chose to see his *Discourse* as 'a paradox rather than a conviction'.[9] Complacently believing that history was on their side, they moved from bewilderment to irritation to hostility, even hatred in the case of Diderot or Voltaire. Yet although they might dismiss him as a 'lunatic', as Voltaire did, they could not help but notice that Rousseau's anti-modernism had struck a responsive chord in many readers. What made him more dangerous was his total lack of any connection with the establishment. On the contrary, he had proved his credentials as a sea-green incorruptible by ostentatiously turning his back on the offer of a royal pension in 1752.[10] His rejection of the Enlightenment had made him *more* radical.

ROUSSEAU'S LOVERS:
FROM A MIMETIC TO AN EXPRESSIVE AESTHETIC

Even the least perceptive of the *philosophes* had to wake up to
the threat when in 1761 Rousseau published an epistolary novel.
The title of the very first edition was *Letters from two lovers
living in a small town at the foot of the Alps* but it soon became
known as *Julie, or The New Héloïse*. Voltaire's reaction that he
would rather kill himself than read such 'a stupid, bourgeois,
impudent and boring' book all the way through was not shared
by the European reading public.[11] By the end of the century it
had gone through more than seventy editions, becoming the
biggest best-seller of the century in the process. When the
printing presses proved unable to keep up with demand, enterprising Parisian booksellers resorted to renting out copies by
the day or even hour.[12] Rousseau was already famous: *La
Nouvelle Héloïse* turned him into a cult. The fan mail which
poured in – and which he carefully preserved – was remarkable
as much for its intensity as for its bulk. Typical was an effusion
from the cavalry captain Jean-Louis Le Cointe, which began
with the apologetic exclamation: 'Yet another letter from
someone unknown to you!' Yet, he went on, so full was his
heart that he had to overcome his reluctance to disturb the
most amiable philosopher of all time. Not only had Rousseau's
book made a case for morality more effectively than any
sermon, he wrote, it had also shown men how they could
achieve earthly happiness.[13]

By pretending to be only the editor of a collection of letters
he had stumbled on, Rousseau sought to give the novel the
kind of immediacy achieved today by the better television soap
operas. His success with only the written word at his disposal

says a great deal for his literary skills, for he was required to assume the guise of several different characters – Julie, the long-suffering and ultimately doomed heroine; her lover, the sensitive Saint-Preux; Lord Edward Bomston, an English nobleman as warm-hearted as he is rich; Wolmar, the noble atheist; and so on. Many of Rousseau's correspondents took him at his word, insisting that the events depicted had really happened and demanding to know what had happened after the end of the book. Not at all untypical was the marquise de Polignac's anguished letter describing her reaction to Julie's death: 'I dare not tell you the effect it made on me. My heart was crushed. Julie dying was no longer an unknown person. I believed I was her sister, her Claire. My seizure became so strong that if I had not put the book away I would have been as ill as those who attended that virtuous woman in her last moments'.[14]

This was not the first time that the tear-ducts of eighteenth-century readers had opened their flood-gates. The sentimental novels of Samuel Richardson, for example, had achieved a similar response in the 1740s. What raised Rousseau's emotional appeal above the ruck was its autobiographical dimension. As he himself observed:

What won me the women's favour was their belief that I had written my own story and that I was myself the hero of my novel. The belief was so firmly established that Mme de Polignac wrote to Mme de Verdelin, begging her to persuade me to let her see Julie's portrait. Everybody was convinced that it was impossible to express feelings so vividly unless one had felt them, or so to depict the raptures of love except with one's own heart as model. In that they were right, and it is true that I wrote the novel in a state of burning ecstasy.[15]

This passage is from Rousseau's *Confessions*, which begins with a programmatic declaration of the primacy of the individual. The opening words are: 'I have resolved on an enterprise which has no precedent, and which, once complete, will have no imitator. My purpose is to display to my kind a portrait in every way true to nature, and the man I shall portray will be myself. Simply myself. I know my own heart and understand my fellow man. But I am made unlike any one I have ever met; I will even venture to say that I am like no one in the whole world. I may be no better, but at least I am different'.[16]

This signalled nothing less than a revolution, one which placed the creator, not the created, at the centre of aesthetic activity. The mimetic view it overturned dated back at least to Plato, who expounded it in Book Ten of *The Republic* through Socrates in conversation with Glaucon, using an everyday object such as a couch as illustration: 'We have these three sorts of couch. There's the one which exists in the natural order of things. This one, I imagine we'd say, was the work of a god ... Then there's the one made by the carpenter ... And then there's the one made by the painter ... Painter, carpenter, god. Three agents responsible for three kinds of couch'. So the painter, poet or any other kind of artist, is twice removed from the ideal couch, that is to say from the truth. Plato also provided a simile to aid understanding of what the artist did, likening him to a man who carried a mirror around with him and was thus able to imitate the external world and all that lived in it.[17]

Subsequent theorists may not have shared Plato's disdain for the arts and those who practised them, but they adhered to the central concept of imitation. Representative of the mainstream of the age of the Enlightenment was Abbé Dubos, hailed by Voltaire in *The Age of Louis XIV* as 'a man of great judgment'.[18] In *Critical Reflections on Poetry and Painting*, first published in 1719 but still being reprinted in the 1750s, he wrote: 'just as a painting imitates the features and colours of nature, so does the musician imitate the sounds, accents, sighs and inflexions of the human voice, together with all the sounds with which nature expresses its feelings and passions'.[19] Imitation did not mean mere copying, of course. Nor did it mean the mechanical reproduction of a specific object. Rather it involved seeking the best elements of nature at its finest ('*la belle nature*') and reproducing them in a painting, sculpture, poem, piece of music or whatever. By selecting and combining natural elements containing beauty, the artist could produce an idealised image more beautiful than nature itself could ever supply. This quest could be assisted by a study of classical Greece and Rome, for it was there that the best examples of idealised beauty could be found, thanks to the superiority of their climate and culture. Hence Winckelmann's famous injunction in his seminal treatise *On the Imitation of the Painting and Sculpture of the Greeks* of 1755: 'there is but one way for the moderns to become great, and perhaps unequalled; I mean by imitating the ancients'.[20]

For neo-classicists such as Winckelmann, the manifest superiority of buildings such as the Parthenon, or statues such as the Apollo Belvedere, revealed the existence of rules governing artistic creation. Moreover, they were rules that could be taught – rules that *should* be taught. In drama there were unities of time and place to be observed, in the visual arts there were the classical proportions to be observed. As Sir Joshua Reynolds put it in 1769: 'I would chiefly recommend, that an implicit obedience to the *Rules of Art*, as established by the practice of the great MASTERS, should be exacted from the *young*

Students. That those models, which have passed through the approbation of ages, should be considered by them as perfect and infallible guides; as subjects for their imitation, not their criticism'.[21] This trenchant advice was delivered in his first discourse to the recently created Royal Academy in London. It was only one of many new creations in the eighteenth century, the century *par excellence* of the art academy. In 1720 there were just nineteen in Europe, of which only four were really operative; by 1790 there were more than a hundred.[22] By this time, it was the academy rather than the master's studio that had become the main centre of instruction for aspiring painters.

The academy was not the sort of environment in which – say – Jean-Jacques Rousseau with his 'mortal aversion to any sort of compulsion'[23] would feel at home. The pedantry could certainly be oppressive. At Vienna, the drawing of foliage was not taught from life but from paper leaves cut and glued together by the professors, for example in 'the spiky oak manner' or 'the rounded lime tree manner'.[24] This was the kind of approach memorably parodied by Wagner in *The Mastersingers of Nuremberg* when the aspiring singer Walther von Stolzing is told he will need to learn the 'writing-paper', 'black-ink', 'hawthorn blossom', 'straw blade' melodies, the 'rose', 'short-lived love' and 'forgotten' tones, and so on and so forth. Well might Friedrich Schiller ask in a letter of 1783: 'do you expect enthusiasm where the spirit of the academies rules?'[25] From the rich stock of dismissive remarks about academies, the following two commend themselves by their pithiness: 'rules are vestal virgins; unless they are violated, there can be no issue' (Johann Georg Hamann) and 'the Aristotelian unities are like crutches for cripples' (Christian Daniel Schubart).[26] The latter remark was a rejoinder to Reynolds' claim in the first discourse that 'rules are only fetters to men of genius'. The most striking rejection of academic authority was delivered by the German artist Asmus Jakob Carstens when he replied to a demand from the Prussian minister of education Karl Friedrich von Heinitz that he return from Rome to resume his teaching duties at the Berlin Academy:

I belong not to the Berlin Academy but to Humanity which has a right to demand of me the highest possible development of my faculties. I shall continue with all my strength to justify myself to the world through my works. Thus I renounce all those benefits, preferring poverty, an uncertain future, and perhaps an infirm and helpless old age, with my body already showing signs of illness, in order to fulfil my duty to humanity and my vocation to art. My capabilities were entrusted to me by God. I must be a faithful steward so that when He says: 'Give a reckoning of thy stewardship', I shall not have to say: 'Lord, the talent with which you entrusted me I have buried in Berlin'.[27]

Carstens died three years later, still in Rome. Stylistically, his art was neo-classical; indeed he has been described as 'the most representative German painter of mature classicism'.[28] Yet he was also aggressively individualistic and vehemently opposed to the academic ethos. Orphaned at fifteen, he passed up the chance to be apprenticed to the famous Johann Heinrich Tischbein, court painter at Kassel, because he could not stomach also being a servant, whose duties would have included standing outside at the rear of the carriage while his master sat inside. So he found himself apprenticed to a cooper instead.[29] In another letter to von Heinitz, Carstens wrote: 'when nature brings forth a genius (and that happens very seldom) and when that genius forces his way past a thousand obstacles into the light of day, then he ought to be supported. Posterity will honour a monarch as much for supporting a genius as for winning a battle or conquering a province'.[30] This kind of comment warns against assuming a contrast between neo-classicism and romanticism based on respective attitudes to academies. For every academician like Reynolds, comfortably nestled in the bosom of the establishment, there was a wild loner like Carstens or Fuseli (of whom more later).[31] Many Enlightenment thinkers who subscribed to mimetic aesthetics doubted the utility of academies. Diderot thought they stifled creativity, while Voltaire commented: 'no work that can be called academic can be called a work of genius, no matter what the genre'.[32]

What proved to be revolutionary was not the rejection of academies, or even rules, but of the whole classical aesthetic based on the imitation of *la belle nature*. As Rousseau demonstrated in *La Nouvelle Héloïse* and *The Confessions*, the truly radical departure was to move from a mimetic aesthetic centred on the work to an *expressive* aesthetic which put the creator at the centre: 'The true object of my confessions is to reveal my inner thoughts exactly in all the situations of my life. It is the history of my soul that I have promised to recount, and to write it faithfully I have need of no other memories; it is enough if I enter again into my inner self, as I have done till now'.[33] This was the essence of the romantic revolution: from now on artistic creativity was to be *from the inside out*. In Hegel's pithy formulation, romanticism was 'absolute inwardness'. Explaining this insight, Hegel observed that romanticism had 'dissolved all particular gods into a pure and infinite self-identity. In this Pantheon all the gods are dethroned, the flame of subjectivity has destroyed them, and instead of plastic polytheism art knows now only *one* God, one spirit, one absolute independence which, as the absolute knowing and willing of itself, remains in free unity with itself'.[34] No longer does the artist carry around a mirror, to hold up to nature. A better metaphor for the creative process is the lamp, which shines from within.[35]

NATURE AND NATURE'S LAWS

The two most quoted lines of poetry about a natural scientist were written by Alexander Pope in 1730:

> Nature and nature's laws lay hid in night,
> God said 'Let Newton be!' and all was light.

They deftly summed up the Enlightenment's view of Newton's greatest achievement among many. By finally destroying the Greek assumption that the celestial and terrestrial worlds are fundamentally different and by demonstrating that both operate according to the same regular, immutable laws of motion, he had opened the way for the mechanisation of heaven and earth. God might still have a place in a post-Newtonian universe but only as the original creator of a mechanism that then ran according to its own laws. In Voltaire's opinion: 'Newton is the greatest man who has ever lived, the very greatest, the giants of antiquity are beside him children playing marbles'.[36] It mattered not that Newton was a devout Christian who wrote extensively on theology and spent a good deal of time trying to unravel the secrets of *The Book of*

Revelation. In the eyes of the *philosophes*, he had delivered the knock-out blow to revealed religion. He had completed the project begun by another English sage, Francis Bacon. It was now clear that the only true form of knowledge is scientific knowledge, that is to say knowledge established by that combination of empiricism and mathematics that is the scientific method, and whatever could not be verified in this way is not knowledge at all.[37] Moreover, science was also opening the way for boundless improvement through the control of nature. As Benjamin Franklin wrote to Joseph Priestley: 'the rapid progress true science now makes, occasions my regretting sometimes that I was born so soon. It is impossible to imagine the height to which may be carried, in a thousand years, the power of man over matter'.[38]

But Rousseau was not the only one to find that the light projected by the Enlightenment illuminated more than it warmed and was bright but not very penetrating. Voltaire himself is reported to have commented: 'I am like a mountain stream: I run fast and bright but not very deep'.[39] As the eighteenth century wore on, a growing number of intellectuals reacted against the elevation of reason to sole eminence. The fundamental charge that the scientific method could explain everything but understand nothing was advanced in many different ways. A universe in which God had been demoted to the role of primal clock-maker seemed to be a chilly place. Johann Heinrich Merck, friend of Goethe and member of the 'storm and stress' [*Sturm und Drang*] group, wrote:

Now we have got the freedom of believing in public nothing but what can be rationally demonstrated. They have deprived religion of all its sensuous elements, that is, of all its relish. They have carved it up into its parts and reduced it to a skeleton without colour and light ... and now it's put in a jar and nobody wants to taste it.[40]

Hamann was more forthright: 'God is a poet, not a mathematician ... What is this much lauded reason with its universalist infallibility, certainty, and over-weening claims, but an *ens rationis* [object of thought], a stuffed dummy ... endowed with divine attributes?'[41] Heinrich von Kleist sneered that all Newton saw in a girl's heart was its cubic capacity and in her breast just a curved line.[42] August Wilhelm Schlegel thought that the limitations of the Enlightenment were best summed up in the question of the mathematician: 'what can a poem prove?'[43] Goethe spoke to God through Mephistopheles in the prologue to *Faust*, which takes place in Heaven:

> The little earth-god still persists in his old ways,
> Ridiculous as ever, as in his first days.
> He'd have improved if you'd not given
> Him a mere glimmer of the light of heaven;
> He calls it Reason, and it only has increased
> His power to be beastlier than a beast.[44]

The Germans were not of course alone in finding rationalism inadequate. The English romantic poets expressed their distaste just as eloquently. In his *Preface* to *Lyrical Ballads* of 1800, William Wordsworth wrote: 'the Man of science seeks truth as a remote and unknown benefactor; he cherishes and loves it in his solitude: the Poet, singing a song in which all human beings join with him, rejoices in the presence of truth as our visible friend and hourly companion'. William Blake was more concise: among the epigrams he attached to his engraving of the classical sculpture group *Laocoön* was: 'Art is the Tree of Life. Science is the Tree of Death'.[45]

He offered a lengthier denunciation in his narrative poem *Milton*:

> The negation is the Spectre, the reasoning power in man:
> This is a false body, an incrustation over my immortal
> Spirit, a selfhood which must be put off and annihilated
> away
> To cleanse the face of my spirit by self examination
> To bathe in the waters of life, to wash off the not human
> I come in self-annihilation and the grandeur of inspiration
> To cast off rational demonstration by faith in the Saviour
> To cast off the rotten rags of memory by inspiration
> To cast off Bacon, Locke, and Newton from Albion's
> covering,
> To take off his filthy garments and clothe him with
> imagination.

Perhaps the most considered criticism of mechanistic natural science came from Coleridge in two letters to his friend Thomas Poole. In 1797 he wrote: 'I have known some who have been rationally educated ... They were marked by a microscopic acuteness, but when they looked at great things, all became blank and they saw nothing'.[46] Four years later he developed this view in a justly celebrated passage that deserves to be quoted in full:

The more I understand of Sir Isaac Newton's works, the more boldly I dare utter to my own mind, and therefore to you, that I believe the souls of five hundred Sir Isaac Newtons would go to the making up of a Shakespeare or a Milton. But if it please the Almighty to grant me health, hope, and a steady mind ..., before my thirtieth year I will thoroughly understand the whole of Newton's works. At present I must content myself with endeavouring to make myself entire master of his easier work, that on Optics. I am exceedingly delighted with the beauty and neatness of his experiments, and with the accuracy of his *immediate* deductions from them; but the opinions founded on these deductions, and indeed his whole theory is, I am persuaded, so exceedingly superficial as without impropriety to be deemed false. Newton was a mere materialist. *Mind*, in his system, is always passive, a lazy Looker-on on an external world.[47]

For Coleridge, Blake and many more romantics, the arch-villain was not, however, Newton but John Locke, for it was his sensationalist psychology that had expelled innate ideas and had thus become 'proposition one of the whole philosophy of the Enlightenment'.[48] At birth, Locke maintained, the human mind was 'white paper, void of all characters, without any ideas'. It acquired knowledge simply and solely through experience – 'in that all our knowledge is founded; and from that it ultimately derives itself'. This rejection of original sin meant a move from a theocentric to an anthropocentric view of life, from God to man. It also opened up boundless possibilities for social engineering. If man was the product of his environment acting on his sensations, then to change the nature of man one only had to change his environment. Coleridge found this epistemology completely unacceptable: the human mind was not passive – 'a lazy Looker-on on an external world' – but active and creative. He prefaced his remarks on Newton in the letter to Poole quoted earlier with the observation: 'My opinion is this – that deep Thinking is attainable only by a man of deep Feeling, and that all Truth is a species of Revelation'. His friend Wordsworth, on the other hand, chose to reinvent Newton as a proto-romantic 'voyaging through strange seas of Thought alone'. Indeed, as Richard Holmes has demonstrated, the natural sciences could be an inspiration to the romantics when approached in a suitably wondering frame of mind'.[49]

Coleridge also advanced another popular critique of empirical science when he referred to Locke as a 'Little-ist'. By that he meant that the critical methodology favoured by rationalist thinkers had dismantled the universe until it lay around them in a meaningless heap of little bits and pieces. As he told Poole: 'they contemplate nothing but *parts* and all *parts* are necessarily little – and the Universe to them is but a mass of little things'.[50] For his part, he explained, he had never lost the habit acquired in childhood through the reading of fairy-stories of seeking knowledge through the imagination. In this way 'my mind has been habituated *to the Vast* & I never regarded *my senses* in any way as the criteria of my belief'. He conceded that this ran the risk of promoting superstition but claimed it was greatly preferable to the alternative: 'are not the Experimentalists credulous even to madness in believing any absurdity, rather than believe the grandest truths, if they have not the testimony of their own senses in their favour?'

Against the 'the cold and lifeless Spitzbergen of armchair reason' (Novalis),[51] the romantics opposed feeling. Again and again they stressed the need to escape from the arid factual world of appearances and enter the interior realm of the self. Caspar David Friedrich warned: 'beware of the superficial knowledge of cold facts, beware of sinful ratiocination, for it kills the heart and when heart and mind have died in a man, there art cannot dwell'.[52] Blake's version of the same thought was: 'Mental Things alone are Real, what is call'd Corporeal. Nobody knows of its Dwelling place; it is Fallacy and its Existence an Imposture'.[53] Goethe's eponymous hero in his best-selling novel *The Sufferings of Young Werther* responded to the 'narrow bounds which confine man's powers of action and investigation' by exclaiming: 'I return into myself, and find a world!'[54] What he found there was a tropical zone far more tempestuous than the icy cliffs of Spitzbergen. Albert, his decent but dull rival for the affections of Lotte, observes primly: 'a person who is carried away by his passions loses all power of deliberation and is as good as drunk or mad'. Werther replies:

Oh, you rationalists! Passion! Drunkenness! Madness! You stand there so calm, so unsympathetic, you moral men! chide the drinker, abhor the irrational, walk past like priests, and like the Pharisee thank God that he has not made you like one of these. I have been drunk more than once, my passions were never far from madness, and I repent of neither: for in my own measure I have learned to understand how it is that all extraordinary beings, who have accomplished something great, something seemingly impossible, have always and necessarily been defamed as drunk and mad.[55]

Shelley made the same point more soberly when he wrote: 'poetry, as has been said, differs in this respect from logic, that it is not subject to the control of the active powers of the mind, and that its birth and recurrence have no necessary connexion with the consciousness or will'.[56]

Underlying these attacks on reason, logic, atomism, materialism and the rest, was a view of nature sharply opposed to that ascribed to Newton. Nothing roused the romantics to greater indignation than the notion that nature was inert matter, to be understood by dissection, experiment and analysis. On the contrary, they proclaimed, all nature constituted a single living organism, a 'Universal Nature or World Soul'. This last concept was central to the philosophy of Friedrich Wilhelm Joseph von Schelling (1775–1854), succinctly summarised by the chiasm 'Nature is visible Spirit; Spirit is invisible Nature'. His own study of physics, medicine and mathematics convinced him that matter consists of an equilibrium of active forces standing in polar opposition to each other, manifesting the 'holy ever-creative, original energy of the World, which generates and busily evolves things out of itself'.[57] The centrality assigned to aesthetic activity in his 'transcendental idealism' made him immensely influential – and popular – with romantic artists, although not all of them imbibed that influence at first hand, preferring the more accessible versions provided by his many admirers. One such was Philipp Otto Runge (1777–1810), whose knowledge of Schelling was probably mediated by the Norwegian scientist and poet Henrik Steffens who wrote about the 'inner life' of the earth.[58] Runge was a painter of great intensity and originality who could also express himself eloquently in writing, as in the following letter to his brother Daniel of 1802:

When above me the sky swarms with countless stars, the wind blusters through the wide space, the wave breaks roaring in the wide night, over the forest the atmosphere reddens, and the sun lights up the world; the valley steams and I throw myself on the grass sparkling with dewdrops. Every leaf and every blade of grass swarms with life, the earth is alive and stirs beneath me, everything rings in one chord, then the soul rejoices and flies in the immeasurable space around me. There is no up and down any more, no time, no beginning and no end. I hear and feel the living breath of God, who holds and carries the world, in whom everything lives and works; here is the highest that we feel – God.[59]

In their different ways, both Turner and Caspar David Friedrich also 'dematerialised nature' (Robert Rosenblum) to reveal its internal powers and mysteries.[60] So nature was no longer Newton's laboratory, but 'Christ's Bible', as Friedrich put it.[61] Like so many other romantics, Friedrich was a Christian pantheist. Commenting on his painting *Swans in Reeds*, he wrote: 'the divine is everywhere, even in a grain of sand; and here I have portrayed it in the reed'.[62] Wordsworth returned to this theme again and again, as in the following lines from *The Excursion*:

> A Herdsman on the lonely mountain-tops,
> Such intercourse was his, and in this sort
> Was his existence oftentimes *possessed*.
> Oh then how beautiful, how bright, appeared
> The written promise! Early had he learned
> To reverence the volume that displays
> The mystery, the life which cannot die;
> But in the mountains did he *feel* his faith.
> All things, responsive to the writing, there
> Breathed immortality, revolving life,
> And greatness still revolving; infinite:
> There littleness was not; the least of things
> Seemed infinite; and there his spirit shaped
> Her prospects, nor did he believe, – he *saw*,
> What wonder if his being thus became
> Sublime and comprehensive![63]

THE CULT OF GENIUS

An important direct influence on Runge was Ludwig Tieck's novel *Franz Sternbald's Wanderings* and its hero's *cri de cœur*: 'not these trees, not these mountains do I wish to copy, but my soul, my mood, which governs me just at this moment'.[64] The inner self was everything: if the light did not shine brightly from within, nothing worthwhile could be achieved. As another great painter of nature, Caspar David Friedrich, put it: 'The artist should not only paint what he sees before him, but also what he sees within him. If, however, he sees nothing within him, then he should also omit to paint that which he sees before him. Otherwise his pictures will resemble those folding screens behind which one expects to find only the sick or even the dead'.[65] And he practised what he preached: in 1816 he recorded: 'for some time I have been idle and felt myself incapable of doing anything. Nothing would flow from inside; the spring had run dry, I was empty; nothing spoke to me from the outside, I was apathetic, and so I concluded that the best thing to do was to do nothing. What is the point of working if it doesn't lead to anything?'[66] A dedicated hiker through the Saxon Riesengebirge, Friedrich spent a great deal of time out in the open air, but when he returned to the studio he excluded the outside world as much as possible. Contemporary pictures of him at work in his studio on the banks of the Elbe at Dresden show the lower half of the window shuttered and only the most essential tools present.[67] His fellow-painter, Wilhelm von Kügelgen, described it as follows: 'Friedrich's studio was so absolutely bare ... It held nothing but the easel, a chair and a table, above which hung the room's only ornament, a T-square, although no one could understand how it came to be so honoured. Even the justifiable paintbox, phials of oil and paint rags were banished to the next room, for Friedrich was of the opinion that all external objects disturb the pictured world within'.[68] Wordsworth made just the same point in 'The Inner Vision':

> If Thought and Love desert us, from that day
> Let us break off all commerce with the Muse:
> With Thought and Love companions of our way –
> Whate'er the senses take or may refuse, –
> The Mind's internal heaven shall shed her dews
> Of inspiration on the humblest lay.

But now that attention had switched to the interior world of individual artists, much sharper differentiation between them was inevitable. However good a painter might be at following the academic rules, if he did not possess the divine spark, what he put on canvas would be boring – not to say worthless. It was no accident that it was during this period that the artist as genius began to set the pace as the role model, not just for fellow-artists but for all society. Of course there had been geniuses recognised in the past, both contemporaries and posterity had venerated Dante, Michelangelo, or Shakespeare, but this was different – now there was a *cult* of genius.[69]

One of the earliest and most influential articulations of this shift was Edward Young's *Conjectures on Original Composition* of 1759. Modern writers had a choice to make, he observed: 'they may soar in the regions of *liberty*, or move in the soft fetters of easy *imitation*'. Young stressed what was to become axiomatic for all romantic creativity – originality: 'Originals are the fairest Flowers: Imitations are of quicker growth, but fainter bloom'.[70] He also offered a definition of genius that is hard to beat: 'What, for the most part, mean we by Genius, but the Power of accomplishing great things without the means generally reputed necessary to that end? A Genius differs from a good Understanding, as a Magician from a good Architect; That raises his structure by means invisible; This by the skilful use of common tools. Hence Genius has ever been supposed to partake of something Divine'.[71] Young was especially fond of contrasting 'learning', which was admirable after its own fashion, and genius: 'Learning we thank, Genius we revere; That gives us pleasure; This gives us rapture; That informs, This inspires; and is itself inspired; for Genius is from Heaven, Learning from man: This sets us above the low, and illiterate; That above the learned and polite. Learning is borrowed knowledge; Genius is knowledge innate, and quite our own'.[72] And of course a genius has no use for rules, which 'like Crutches, are a needful Aid to the Lame, tho' an Impediment to the Strong. A Homer casts them away'.[73]

In his native England, Young's treatise made little impact at first, but it was quickly taken up in Germany, where it appeared in two different translations within two years of publication.[74] No one responded with greater – or more influential – enthusiasm than Johann Georg Hamann, the self-styled 'Magus of the North'.[75] Hamann had good first-hand knowledge of the English intellectual world, having lived in London during 1757–8. It was there that he experienced an intense religious conversion which inspired him to develop a highly individual world-view. The entire classical inheritance he abandoned. In *Socratic Memorabilia*, published in 1759, he asked what permitted Homer to be ignorant of the rules or Shakespeare to disregard them. His one-word answer was:

'genius'. Moreover, the prerequisites of genius were originality, passion and enthusiasm: 'passion alone gives hands, feet and wings to abstractions and hypotheses; gives spirit, life and voice to images and symbols'.[76]

Hamann's 'polemical pyrotechnics', as Nicholas Boyle has dubbed them,[77] were too incoherent and opaque to inspire a movement. It was through his pupil, Johann Gottfried Herder, and Herder's friend Goethe, that his insights entered the mainstream. In his autobiography Goethe recorded Hamann's huge influence on everyone who found the prevailing *Zeitgeist* uncongenial and also paid tribute to his 'wonderful greatness and profundity' [*Großheit und Innigkeit*].[78] Goethe's own epiphany occurred at Strassburg in 1770, brought on by the overwhelming impact of its Gothic cathedral. He articulated his response in 'Concerning German Architecture', an essay dedicated to Erwin von Steinbach, the cathedral's chief architect, and published in a collection edited by Herder in 1773. Goethe emphatically rejected any idea that beauty could be found by joining schools, adopting principles or following rules: they were so many chains enslaving insight and energy. In the essay's key passage Goethe defined his alternative: 'The only true art is characteristic art. If its influence arises from deep, harmonious, independent feeling, from feeling peculiar to itself, oblivious, yes, ignorant of everything foreign, then it is whole and living, whether it be born from crude savagery or cultured sentiment'.[79] Untamed, spontaneous authenticity was everything: 'for a genius, principles are even more harmful than examples'.[80]

In developing his new aesthetic, Goethe was also strongly influenced by Rousseau. In the year following the latter's death in 1778, he made a pilgrimage to the island of Saint Pierre on the lake of Bienne in Switzerland, where Rousseau had taken refuge after his expulsion from Geneva. There Goethe wrote his name on the wall of the room the fugitive had occupied. He also took the opportunity to visit some of the places where episodes from *La Nouvelle Héloïse* had been set – and was duly overcome by tearful emotion. Shortly after the posthumous publication of *The Confessions* in 1782, Goethe was given a copy by his mother, as part of a lavish new edition of Rousseau's collected works, and enthused: 'even the few pages at which I have looked are like shining stars; imagine several volumes like that! What a heavenful! What a gift to mankind a noble human being is!'[81] In Rousseau's *Dictionary of Music*, first published in 1768, Goethe would have found the following emotional effusion under the entry 'GENIUS':

Seek not, young artist, what meaning is expressed by genius. If you are inspired with it, you must feel it in yourself. Are you destitute of it, you will never be acquainted with it. The genius of a musician submits the whole universe to his art. He paints every piece by sounds; he gives a language even to silence itself; he renders ideas by sentiments; sentiments by accents; and the passions which he expresses are drawn from the bottom of the heart. Voluptuousness, by his assistance, receives fresh charms; the grief to which he gives utterance, excites cries; he continually is burning, and he never consumes.[82]

Indeed, Rousseau's influence on German intellectuals was immense, far greater than on their equivalents in France, where it was only after 1789 that he achieved recognition for his political works. Johann Heinrich Campe had 'My Saint!' inscribed on a bust of Rousseau; Herder's fiancée Caroline

Flachsland learned French expressly to read the works of 'a saint and a prophet'; Herder invoked, 'Come Rousseau, and be my guide!'; Friedrich Maximilian Klinger believed that Rousseau had brought 'a new revelation' to the world; and so on and so forth. No less a figure than Kant wrote that it was Rousseau who had put him right again [*hat mich wieder zurecht gemacht*].[83]

THE ELEVATION OF THE ARTIST
AND THE SACRALISATION OF ART

This elevation of genius, which became a permanent feature of the modern cultural landscape, had important consequences for the status of the creative artist. By 1800 'genius' had ceased to be one characteristic among many that an individual might possess and had progressed to encompass the whole person: *avoir du génie* means just to possess exceptional talent; *être un génie* is to be superhuman.[84] His – and the gender-specific possessive pronoun can be used here without apology – emergence was greatly assisted by the secularisation of European society and the simultaneous sacralisation of its culture. If the eighteenth century was 'the age of faith' as well as 'the age of reason', it also witnessed a downgrading of organised religion and its priests. For a growing number of educated Europeans, both traditional doctrines and traditional institutions were no longer sufficient. They looked to art in all its various forms to fill the transcendental gap that was opening up.

It was however a special kind of art: art that was serious, profound (at least in intention), and above all self-contained. It was around this time that 'art' acquired its modern meaning.

For Dr Johnson, 'art' still chiefly meant skill, as in 'the art of boiling sugar', and even in his subordinate definition of 'a science, as the liberal arts', the main emphasis was on 'the power of doing something not taught by nature and instinct; as, to *walk* is natural, to *dance* is an art'.[85] A generation later, art had advanced to become the supreme form of human activity. It could no longer be subordinate to some external patron such as a prince or a church or designed simply to entertain. So the exponents of a sacralised art rejected not just the triumphalism of Versailles and the ecclesiastical art of the baroque but also the hedonism of the rococo. Particularly influential was Winckelmann, who in effect created an aesthetic religion by marrying the language of Pietist introspection to sensualist paganism. Winckelmann's account of the Apollo Belvedere is more than an appreciation of a statue, it is a religious exercise, because for him the statue does not represent God, it *is* a God.[86] Yet for all his emotionalism, Winckelmann was operating very much within a neoclassical framework; indeed his celebrated call for 'noble simplicity and calm grandeur' represents the best summary of its programme. It was only when the last external restraints were cast aside that the creative artist could break out of the mimetic cocoon and achieve full independence as a high priest of an aesthetic religion.

For this new kind of purpose, a new kind of space was needed. Sacralised art could no longer be satisfied with sharing churches or palaces with prelates or princes but demanded its own temples. An early example was the opera house on Unter den Linden in Berlin, commissioned by Frederick II of Prussia as soon as he came to the throne in 1740. Taking the form of an autonomous classical temple, it was the first free-standing opera house in Europe.[87] The inscription above the portico proclaimed '*Fridericus Rex Apollini et Musis*' – 'Dedicated by King Frederick to Apollo and the Muses'. It was no coincidence that Frederick reviled Christianity as a tissue of pernicious fictions and turned instead to the arts to satisfy his need for transcendental experience: 'since my childhood I have loved the arts, literature and the sciences, and if I can contribute to their propagation, I dedicate myself with all the zeal at my disposal, because there can be no true happiness in this world without them'.[88] His aestheticism was shared by another great German role-model, Goethe, who wrote after visiting the art gallery of the Elector of Saxony at Dresden: 'this sanctuary ... imparted a unique feeling of solemnity which much resembled the sensation with which one enters a church, as the adornments of so many temples, the objects of so much adoration, seemed to be displayed here only for art's sacred ends'.[89]

Now installed in their own buildings – the first free-standing museum in Europe was the Museum Fridericianum in Kassel, constructed between 1769 and 1779 to contain the collections and library of Landgrave Frederick II – paintings could be worshipped in their own right. More or less simultaneously, music found its own autonomous space in the public concerts that mushroomed during the second half of the eighteenth century. As they moved from tavern to dedicated concert-hall, they required a more reverential attitude from the audience. This was well put by Fanny Burney's heroine Evelina in the novel of that name published in 1778:

About eight o'clock we went to the Pantheon. I was extremely struck with the beauty of the building, which greatly surpassed whatever I could have expected or imagined. Yet, it has more the appearance of a chapel, than of a place of diversion; and, though I was quite charmed with the magnificence of the room, I felt that I could not be as gay and thoughtless there as at Ranelagh [a pleasure garden], for there is something in it which rather inspires awe and solemnity, than mirth and pleasure.[90]

This image of the concert-hall as church and the concert as divine service became a recurring feature of romanticism. In 'The remarkable musical life of the composer Joseph Berglinger', published as part of the enormously influential *Heartfelt Effusions of an Art-loving Monk* of 1796, Wilhelm Heinrich Wackenroder and Ludwig Tieck recorded: 'when Joseph went to an important concert, he avoided looking at the glamorous audience and sat by himself in a corner, listening with devotion as if he were in a church – silent and motionless, his eyes fixed on the ground in front of him'.[91]

The secularisation of society, intensified by the French Revolution, urbanisation and industrialisation, encouraged the sacralisation of art in all its forms. In 1832 the French periodical *L'Artiste* asserted: 'in our nineteenth century, a century that no longer believes anything, music has become a kind of religion, a last belief to which society is clinging with all its might, exhausted as it is by dogmas and words'.[92] Although an exaggeration, even if applied only to Paris, it was not an aberration. Of the many supporting observations from contemporaries, the following by Hermione Quinet about the period before 1848 is representative: 'I often forget that the Conservatoire is not a church, that the hundred musicians in the *Société des Concerts* live scattered throughout the twenty arrondissements of Paris and not in a seminary, that they are not a college of priests gathered before us to perform a holy service each Sunday'.[93]

Especially revealing were the events following Beethoven's death on 26 March 1827. The funeral oration, written by the leading poet of the day, Franz Grillparzer, and delivered at the gates of the Währing cemetery in Vienna by the leading classical actor of the day, Heinrich Anschütz, did not mention the Christian God once. The deity to whom Grillparzer – and Beethoven – paid homage was Art: 'the thorns of life had wounded him deeply, and as the castaway clings to the shore, so did he seek refuge in thine arms, O thou glorious sister and peer of the Good and the True, thou balm of wounded hearts, heaven-born Art!'[94] Beethoven's role as secular redeemer was well put in a poem dedicated to his memory by Schubert's friend Gabriel Seidl: 'He teaches us new jubilation, new laments, new prayer and new jests'. Anticipating Richard Wagner's celebrated injunction to emotionalise the intellect, Seidl added: 'He feels through his mind; he thinks through his heart'.[95]

In the popular imagination, Beethoven was the romantic hero *par excellence*: the lonely, tortured, afflicted, uncompromising, utterly original genius, a man who 'treated God as an equal', as his friend Bettina von Arnim recorded.[96] In his autobiography, Richard Wagner recorded that when he was fourteen he had been bowled over when first hearing a Beethoven symphony (the 7th) at the Gewandhaus in Leipzig, with 'the added impact of Beethoven's physiognomy, as shown by lithographs of the time, as well as the knowledge of his deafness and his solitary and withdrawn life. There soon arose in me an image of the highest supernal originality, beyond comparison with anything'.[97] Franz Liszt claimed that for *all* musicians 'Beethoven's work is like the pillar of cloud and fire which guided the Israelites through the desert – a pillar of cloud to guide us by day, a pillar of fire to guide us by night "so that we may progress both day and night".[98]

Liszt provided material evidence of his enthusiasm when he intervened to save the faltering project to erect a statue of Beethoven at his birthplace, Bonn, in 1845. Although the organisation was chaotic, to put it very mildly, the event supplied the best possible evidence of Beethoven's posthumous standing. Tens of thousands of enthusiasts poured into the small Rhenish city for the celebrations, including Berlioz, Meyerbeer, Spohr, Charles Hallé, Jenny Lind and an army of journalists and critics. That this was much more than a musical event was dramatised by the appearance of Queen Victoria, Prince Albert and the King and Queen of Prussia, not to mention the launching of a steamboat named *Ludwig van Beethoven* on the opening day. In his speech at the ceremonial banquet, Liszt described the journeys made to Bonn from all over Europe by the participants as constituting one great pilgrimage.[99]

Apart from his supreme skills as a pianist, Liszt was also a prolific writer, contributing frequently to the musical periodicals on a wide range of topics. In a remarkable series of articles entitled 'On the situation of artists and their social condition', published in instalments in the *Gazette musicale de Paris* in 1835, he delivered a passionate critique of modern civilisation. Its degeneration, he argued, was due to the separation of religion, politics, art and the natural sciences into separate activities. Only when they could be reunited under the aegis of the arts, especially music, could man's alienation be resolved. It was high time that creative artists realised that they had a 'great religious and social MISSION' [*sic*].[100] To the poet

Ludwig Eckardt, he wrote: 'art is for us none other than the mystic ladder from earth to Heaven – from the finite to the Infinite – from mankind to God: an everlasting inspiration and impulse towards redemption through love!'[101]

As art was sacralised and placed on a pedestal, so were its creators elevated to become high-priests of this aesthetic religion. As early as 1802 Joseph Haydn had referred to himself as 'a not wholly unworthy priest of this sacred art'.[102] By the middle of the nineteenth century, the use of quasi-religious language to describe the musician's calling was common, as for example when an English periodical referred to Mendelssohn and Spohr as 'high priests of art who wield the sceptre by right of intellectual power' or when Prince Schwarzenberg, one of the greatest aristocrats of the Habsburg Empire, praised Liszt as 'a true prince of music, a genuine *grand seigneur* ... a priest of art'.[103] This kind of tribute was not confined to musicians, although they were especially venerated. In 1842 Elizabeth Barrett Browning was moved by Benjamin Haydon's portrait of 'Wordsworth on Helvellyn' to write:

> Wordsworth upon Helvellyn! Let the cloud
> Ebb audibly along the mountain-wind,
> Then break against the rock, and show behind
> The lowland valleys floating up to crowd
> The sense with beauty. He, with forehead bowed
> And humble-lidded eyes, as one inclined
> Before the sovran thought of his own mind;
> And very meek with inspirations proud,
> Takes here his rightful place as poet-priest
> By the high-altar, singing prayer and prayer
> To the higher Heavens.[104]

The poet as priest: Benjamin Haydon, Wordsworth on Helvellyn
(1842)

THE PHILISTINE PUBLIC

The priests of art themselves welcomed their elevation, of course, not least because it offered an escape from a dilemma created by the rapid expansion of the public sphere. It was in the course of the eighteenth century that the inter-related expansions of population, the economy, towns and literacy combined to create a new source of patronage. Increasingly, especially in the great metropolises such as London and Paris, writers, artists and musicians were able to dispense with royal, aristocratic or ecclesiastical patronage. The ability of Alexander Pope to live solely from the sale of his publications – 'indebted to no prince or peer alive', as he put it[105] – was very exceptional in the first quarter of the century, but would have been less so by the last. Mozart did well as a free-lance musician in Vienna after 1781, at least until the Turkish War of 1788 and the illness of his wife caused temporary difficulties.[106]

The public provided not just a new source of income but also a new source of legitimacy. As the various media and institutions of the public sphere – newspapers, periodicals, coffee-houses, art exhibitions, concerts, literary societies, reading clubs, and the like – expanded, so did the awareness of a new cultural (and political) arbitrator. For this was very much a perceived change. In 1782 Louis Sébastien Mercier wrote in his periodical *Tableau de Paris*:

During the past thirty years a great and significant revolution has occurred in the way we think. Today public opinion enjoys a power in Europe which is preponderant and irresistible. ... It is men of letters who deserve the credit, for in the recent past it is they who have formed public opinion in a number of very important crises. Thanks to their efforts, public opinion has exercised a decisive influence on the course of events. And it also seems that they are creating a national spirit.[107]

Unfortunately, the anonymous public could be just as demanding as any prince or prelate. Members of the public knew what they liked. And just like any Medici or Habsburg, when they paid the piper they expected to call the tune. For the artist, the trick was to take their money and adulation without having to compromise creative freedom. Not easy to do at the best of times, this balancing-act became progressively more difficult as the public broadened in numbers without deepening in appreciation. A Haydn symphony was one thing, Beethoven's 9th was quite another. What the public wanted was easy-listening: plenty of variety, good tunes, regular rhythms, not too long, and all preferably in easy keys so that it could be played at home on the piano that was increasingly becoming a feature of middle-class parlours.[108] Ironically, this kind of 'cultural retardation', which affected all the other arts too, came when technological changes such as lithography, the steam-driven printing press, and mass production that brought down prices, were bringing more varied, higher-quality but cheaper artefacts to market.[109]

The way out of this dilemma, to avoid jumping from the frying-pan of aristocratic tyranny into the fire of public vulgarity, was to liberate art from both the scum and the dregs of society and to place it on an altar in unsullied eminence (mixing the metaphor once more). So artists of all genres embraced with enthusiasm the sacralisation preached by the aestheticians. From the rich range of examples available, the following three recommend themselves by their eloquence and relative brevity. First, Novalis:

Whoever feels unhappy in this world, whoever fails to find what he seeks – then let him enter the world of books, art and nature, this eternal domain which is both ancient and modern simultaneously, and let him live there in this secret church of a better world. There he will surely find a lover and a friend, a fatherland and a God.[110]

Secondly, Keats with the opening lines of *Endymion*:

> A thing of beauty is a joy for ever:
> Its loveliness increases; it will never
> Pass into nothingness; but still will keep
> A bower quiet for us, and a sleep
> Full of sweet dreams, and health, and quiet breathing.

And finally, Goethe:

True poetry identifies itself as such by knowing how to liberate us from the earthly burdens that oppress us, by being a secular gospel, by creating inner cheerfulness and outward contentment. Like a hot-air balloon, it raises us into the higher regions and gives us a bird's-eye view of the confused labyrinths of the world.[III]

Goethe had parted company with revealed religion at a very early age, but it was not only unbelievers who were attracted by sacralised art. Novalis was a devout Christian, as was Franz Liszt, who even entered minor orders and was known as the 'Abbé Liszt'. They did not see devotion to art as a substitute for faith, rather as part and parcel of the same exercise. As Liszt put it: 'one should always and only speak of divine art; and if people are taught from their early years onwards that God has given them reason, free will and conscience, one should always add: and Art – for Art is the truly divine!'[112]

Of all the creative artists, the musicians found this easiest, for their medium speaks directly to the psyche without any mediating word or image. This was put particularly well by Leonard Willoughby: 'The romanticists (*sic*) hoped to reach ultimate reality through music because, through the quasi-identity of its form and content, it seemed to derive from the eternal primordial chaos without having passed first through the ordering faculty of the human mind. It was precisely this Dionysiac element in music which the romanticists loved and stressed'.[113] It did not mean that they were obliged to retreat to some remote ivory tower, removed from the grubby tastes of the general public. It was rather that sacralisation provided a self-protective detachment from the worst excesses of the market-place.

When Friedrich Schiller escaped from what he saw as the tyrannical regime of the Duke of Württemberg, he made a resounding declaration of independence:

I write as a citizen of the world who serves no prince. From now on all my ties are dissolved. The public is now everything to me, my preoccupation, my sovereign and my friend. Henceforth I belong to it alone. I wish to place myself before this tribunal and no other. It is the only thing I fear and respect. A feeling of greatness comes over me with the idea that the only fetter I wear is the verdict of the world – and that the only throne I shall appeal to is the human soul.[114]

That was in 1784. A decade later he had entered the service of the Duke of Saxony-Weimar, had turned decisively against his former 'sovereign and friend', and was developing a theory of sacralised aesthetics that was as elitist as could be. Beethoven, who was a great admirer of Schiller, shared his disdain, criticising Rossini for giving the public what they wanted and exclaiming to Hummel, 'It is said *vox populi, vox dei* – I never believed it'.[115] His own disciple, Berlioz, agreed: 'the stultification of the majority of the public, its lack of understanding in matters of imagination and the heart, its love of brilliant platitudes, the vulgarity of all its melodic and rhythmic instincts, have of necessity driven the performers along the road they now follow'.[116] Now that it was the artist who mattered most, rather than what he created, the response of the audience was of no consequence. In his celebrated review of Johann Georg Sulzer's classical aesthetic, first published in 1772, Goethe concluded: 'the only thing that matters is the artist, that he should experience the joys of life only in his art and that he should live immersed in his medium with all his emotions and powers. Who cares about the gawping public and whether, once it has done its gawping, it can or cannot give an account of why it has gawped?'[117]

This was an attitude shared by the English romantic poets, among whom Tom Moore complained about the 'lowering of standards that must necessarily arise from the extending of the circle of judges'. Keats declared: 'I have not the slightest feel of humility towards the Public' and Shelley advised: 'accept no counsel from the simple-minded; time reverses the judgement of the foolish crowd'. Wordsworth castigated anyone 'who can believe that there is anything of divine infallibility in the clamour of that small though loud portion of the community, ever governed by factitious influence, which, under the name of the public, passes itself upon the unthinking, for the people'.[118]

In a word, the public was philistine. It was no coincidence that it was during this period that 'philistine' acquired its modern meaning as 'an uneducated or unenlightened person; one perceived to be indifferent or hostile to art or culture, or whose interests and tastes are commonplace or material; a person who is not a connoisseur', defined by the *Oxford English*

Dictionary. In this sense it was the invention of German students, who took it from the funeral oration delivered at Jena in 1668 following the death of one of their number at the hands of a local burgher. The preacher's text was taken from the Old Testament: 'The Philistines be upon thee, Samson' (Judges, xvi:9). Henceforth, the students identified themselves with Samson and the townspeople as the philistines. By *c.* 1800 the confrontation had expanded from town versus gown to intellectuals versus the rest of society, especially middle-class society.

Long before Mr Gradgrind made his appearance in Charles Dickens' *Hard Times* in 1854, his stereotype was established as the European intelligentsia's *bête noire*. They chose to believe that everyone engaged in mundane business was motivated solely by considerations of utility while they themselves were inspired solely by devotion to art. In Ludwig Tieck's novel *Franz Sternbald's Wanderings* of 1798 the hero angrily rejects the observations made by a craftsman and a businessman that the arts are useless and artists silly idiots:

And what do you mean by utility? Must absolutely everything come down to just eating, drinking and clothing? ... I say it once again: everything that is truly elevated cannot and must not be judged by its utility; having to be useful is completely alien to art's divine nature and to insist that it be so is to strip what should be sublime of its nobility and to debase it to the level of the basic needs of humanity. Of course man needs lots of different things, but his spirit must not be degraded to become the servant of his body – the servant of his servant in other words. Like any good head of a household, he must attend to material needs, but must not allow this concern to be his be-all and end-all. Art is the guarantee of our immortality.[119]

Tieck was twenty-five years old when his book was published. Although romantic contempt for the mundane world of the money-grubbing philistines was not confined to angry young men and women, it was certainly expressed by them with special vehemence. A good example was provided by Clemens Brentano's 'oration against the philistines', delivered at Jena at the end of 1799 when he was twenty-one. The little Thuringian university-town had become the centre of German romanticism, for at the house of August Wilhelm Schlegel (aged 32) and his wife Caroline (36) there gathered his brother Friedrich (27), Fichte (37), Schelling (24), Tieck and Brentano. Another frequent visitor was the Saxon mining official Friedrich von Hardenberg (27), better known as the poet 'Novalis'. Brentano's essential charge against the philistines was that they were boring and limited, looking for nothing in their lives beyond domesticity, security, peace and order – 'a philistine can never wish to become a tight-rope walker' was his withering comment.[120] This sort of attitude was not confined to the Germans. Théophile Gautier wrote in his preface to *Mademoiselle de Maupin* (1835): 'Only what is useless is truly beautiful; everything that is useful is ugly, for it is the expression of some need, and the needs of men are ignoble and disgusting, his nature being what it is, inferior and infirm'.[121]

A more philosophical answer to the Gradgrinds of late eighteenth-century Germany (and there were plenty of them about) was provided by Friedrich Schiller. Art was not a peripheral activity, he argued, but absolutely central to human existence: 'human beings only play when they are in the full sense of the word human and *they are only fully human when they play*'.[122] Now that the French Revolution had shown the bankruptcy of political solutions, by inflicting state terror, war and imperialist conquest, the only way forward lay through aesthetics: 'if man is ever to solve the problem of politics in practice, he will have to approach it through the problem of the aesthetic, because it is only through Beauty that man makes his way to freedom'.[123] His friend Goethe mercilessly satirised the philistine in *Wilhelm Meister's Apprenticeship* (1795–6) in the person of Wilhelm's brother-in-law Werner, who issues the following advice: 'here is my joyous credo: conduct your business, acquire money, enjoy yourself with your family, and don't bother about anybody else unless you can use them to your advantage'.[124] But Wilhelm wants to be an actor and is not listening. Goethe returned to the theme in Part One of *Faust*, through Wagner, Faust's pedantic secretary, who believes in the utility of factual knowledge:

> Oh dear, what can one do,
> Sitting day after day among one's books!
> The world's so distant, and one never looks
> Even through a spyglass at it; so how can
> One learn to bring about the betterment of man?

To which Faust replies:

> Give up pursuing eloquence, unless
> You can speak as you feel! One's very heart
> Must pour it out, with primal power address
> One's hearers and compel them with an art
> Deeper than words.
> But what can blend all hearts into a whole?
> Only the language of the soul.[125]

Goethe had begun to write *Faust* in the 1770s. By the time the first part was published in 1808, he was feeling increasingly out of step with the younger generation of German writers. In the course of the 1780s he had turned away from his 'storm and stress' days, moving to an aesthetic that was more classical than romantic. As he grew older, so did his distaste for the latter intensify. In a famous conversation with his friend Eckermann in 1829, he went so far as to apostrophise classicism as 'health' and romanticism as 'disease'.[126] Shortly after Goethe died three years later, Part Two of *Faust* was published. The ending might suggest that Faust had succumbed to the utilitarian ethos of the philistines. For what prompts him to say 'Beautiful moment, do not pass away!', and thus to lose his wager with Mephistopheles, is the prospect of a successful land reclamation scheme.[127] Yet this concern for the physical world is accompanied by that sense of individual struggle with which Faust (and Goethe too, for the work is the most important single part of his 'great confession') began his quest. Immediately prior to his expression of satisfaction, Faust had proclaimed:

> Yes! To this vision I am wedded still,
> And this as wisdom's final word I teach:
> Only that man earns freedom, merits life,
> Who must reconquer both in constant daily strife.
> In such a place, by danger still surrounded,
> Youth, manhood, age, their brave new world have founded.
> I long to see that multitude and stand
> With a free people on free land!

Germans were especially sensitive to philistinism because

there were no metropolitan centres anywhere in German-speaking Europe. Even Vienna (with a population of about 225,000 in 1800) and Berlin (175,000) were dwarfed by London or Paris, which were four or five times larger. Pre-industrial Germany was a land of small towns and small-town attitudes.[128] For this paradoxical reason, it proved to be in the van of romantic developments. In France it was not until the 1830s that the word '*art*' came into general use to denote art *per se*. Previously, it had been used to denote a specific form and was accompanied by a descriptive adjective, as in '*art musical*' or '*beaux-arts*'. This was partly a reaction to the 'industrialised literature' (the title of an article by Sainte-Beuve) that appeared to be debasing aesthetic standards. Particular exception was taken to the serialised novels that became enormously popular during the 1830s and the new emphasis on productivity. When criticised for his over-elaborate style, Charles Nodier rejoindered that an eight-syllable word made up a line – and for each line he was paid a franc.[129]

Against this, the romantics opposed the notion of '*l'art pour l'art*' or 'art for art's sake'. There is some dispute as to who coined the phrase first, but the most likely candidate seems to have been Henry Crabb Robinson, an English nonconformist who spent many years in Germany consorting with leading intellectuals, including Goethe, Schiller and the Schlegels. Early in 1804 he was visited at Weimar by Benjamin Constant, who recorded in his *Journal intime* on 10 February: 'I have a conversation with Robinson, a pupil of Schelling. His work on Kant's *Aesthetics* contains some very energetic ideas. Art for art's sake, without any purpose, for every kind of purpose distorts [*dénature*] art'.[130] In other words, this was a German idea, turned into a slogan by an

Englishman and recorded by a Frenchman.

Perhaps because '*l'art pour l'art*' sounds so much more mellifluous than 'art for art's sake' or '*Kunst um der Kunst willen*', it turned out to have a special resonance in France. Victor Cousin used the phrase in a course of lectures delivered in 1818 shortly after a visit to Germany. Eventually he published them in book form as *On the True, the Beautiful and the Good* (1836) stating: 'art can no more serve religion or morality than what is pleasing or useful ... Religion must be for religion's sake, morality for morality's sake and art for art's sake ... Let us absorb this idea, that art itself is a kind of religion. God manifests himself to us through the idea of the true, the good and the beautiful'.[131] Following the July Revolution of 1830, Gautier emphatically rejected any idea that art should have a political role: 'it is neither red nor white nor even tricolour; it is nothing and is only aware of revolutions when the bullets break the windows'. A poem served nothing but beauty, he added – how could it be otherwise, for 'in general as soon as something becomes useful, it ceases to be beautiful'.[132] As we shall see in Chapter Three, not all romantics – and especially not French romantics – agreed that romanticism had no political complexion.

This kind of aestheticism had a special appeal to musicians and those who wrote about music. Stendhal (the *nom de plume* of Henri Beyle) was too fond of irony to be included among the romantics, but he shared many of their attitudes. In his *Life of Rossini* (1823), he wrote: 'society itself, or at least nineteen parts out of twenty of that society, including everything that is vulgar and bourgeois, turns and turns again about one axis: vanity'. It was just the sort of cultural environment, he observed, in which a lightweight and meretricious talent such as Rossini could flourish: 'light, lively, amusing, never wearisome, but seldom exalted – Rossini would appear to have been brought into this world for the express purpose of conjuring up visions of ecstatic delight in the commonplace soul of the Average Man'. In particular, Rossini's music appealed to 'the philistine section of the audience ... [which] demands primarily the ornamentation which it has *grown to expect*'. He concluded the book with the observation that Paris was not just the centre of European civilisation but also the capital of philistinism: 'if you promise to keep a secret, I might whisper in your ear that Rossini's style is the musical embodiment, not so much of France as of *Paris*: it is not really merry, but it is supremely vain and excitable; it is never passionate, but always witty; and if it is never boring, it is very, *very* rarely sublime'.[133]

The distinguished French critic Joseph d'Ortigue, who among other things wrote the first biography of his friend Berlioz, agreed. He satirised the philistine bourgeois in the shape of a lady from the fashionable Chaussée d'Antin who gave her a daughter a piano and music lessons in the same sort of spirit that she gave her son a coat and herself a cashmere jacket, because she regards music simply 'as an item of fashion and vanity'.[134] Also nodding his head in approval was Franz Liszt, for whom Paris was a base for almost thirty years. In an article in a musical periodical in 1835, he wrote that at private gatherings to which he was admitted, although 'only an artist', he sat depressed by the 'ignorant silence' that greeted a work by one of the great masters while some wretched bagatelle was rewarded with rapture.[135] It was no different in other musical centres, as Liszt found when he went to Milan to give a recital at La Scala. What the public there liked best was a medley drawn from familiar operas, during which they joined in whistling and humming the tunes. When he tried to raise the level with a more challenging piece, a member of the audience shouted out, 'I come to the theatre for entertainment not instruction!'[136]

This was a necessary result of the expansion of the public sphere. More and more people were feeling obliged to present themselves as cultured, but the culture they embraced seemed to be increasingly debased. Representative of the disdain felt by the artistic community was the description of the musical taste of the typical bourgeois offered by a Parisian periodical in 1843. Now that he had made a bit of money, he had traded up culturally, abandoning the barrel-organ he used to like. Now he bought the latest album of 'romances' and liked to have them played at home on the piano to show what a great music-lover he is: 'his daughter has a piano, that goes without saying, and of course a good and expensive one, so that he can boast "That's a fine instrument I've got there, better than anything the English manufacturers can turn out – I had to give three thousand francs for it"'. The bourgeois dismissed any music that was beyond him as 'learned' (*savant*), preferring short pieces written for the piano, medleys of arias from comic operas and especially quadrilles. So far as the other arts were concerned, he liked his paintings to be '*bien fondue*', by which he meant portraits of people with pink complexions, sentimental paintings or genre scenes. He liked his architecture to be covered with sculpture, 'because if the buildings are well-covered one can see that one has got something for one's money'. In short, the anonymous author concluded, the intelligentsia believes that the bourgeois has no understanding of beauty and likes only what is vulgar and stupid.[137]

*

When charting the progress of the romantic revolution, there is a natural tendency to follow the example set by its supporters of over-simplifying the opposition. In reality, the Enlightenment was a house with many mansions, with some members occupying more than one simultaneously. What could seem more blithely optimistic than the following celebrated passage from Pope's *Essay on Man*?

> All nature is but Art, unknown to thee;
> All Chance, Direction, which thou canst not see;
> All Discord, Harmony not understood.
> All partial Evil, universal Good:
> And, spite of Pride, in erring Reason's spite,
> One truth is clear, Whatever is, is right.[138]

Those lines were published in 1733. Four years later, in his imitation of the second epistle of the second book of Horace, Alexander Pope congratulated a friend who claimed to have conquered avarice, but went on:

> I wish you joy, sir, of a tyrant gone;
> But does no other lord it at this hour,
> As wild and mad: the avarice of power?
> Does neither rage inflame, nor fear appal?
> Not the black fear of death, that saddens all?
> With terrors round, can Reason hold her throne,
> Despise the known, nor tremble at the unknown?
> Survey both worlds, intrepid and entire,
> In spite of witches, devils, dreams, and fire?[139]

In a world in which the light shone by Newton still left

many dark patches, there were plenty of irrational eruptions to sustain this more pessimistic view of life. The most spectacular occurred at 9.30 a.m. on 1 November 1755 when a devastating earthquake struck Lisbon. Many of the buildings left standing were then destroyed by a great tsunami, if they lay near the waterfront, or by fire if they were further inland. The loss of life and suffering were commensurate. The Lisbon earthquake was not the worst that had ever been, but it was certainly the most publicised. This was chiefly due to the colossal impact of Voltaire's 'Poem on the Lisbon Disaster', dashed off before the end of the month. It went through a score of editions during the following year, unleashing a torrent of pamphlets for and against.[140]

Even more influential was the treatment in *Candide*, published in 1759, probably the most read of all Voltaire's works and one of the two or three biggest sellers of the century. As the only three survivors of a shipwreck, Candide, Dr Pangloss and a brutal sailor struggle ashore at Lisbon just as the earthquake strikes. Candide exclaims that the end of the world must have come, the sailor rushes off in search of plunder, while Dr Pangloss asks, 'What can be the sufficing reason for this phenomenon?' in accordance with his guiding principle that 'all is for the best in this best of all possible worlds'. In the person of the incorrigibly optimistic doctor, Voltaire was satirising Leibniz in particular and more generally the view that 'whatever is, is right'. So Pangloss upbraids the pillaging, whoring, drunken sailor with the words 'Friend, this is not right. You trespass against the universal reason, and abuse your time'. He also consoles the survivors with the cheering message that 'all this is for the best, since, if there is a volcanic eruption at Lisbon, then it could not have occurred in any other spot.

It is impossible that things should be elsewhere than where they are; for everything is good'.[141]

Poor Candide and Pangloss have many trials and tribulations to endure before finally coming to rest on a small farm near Constantinople. In this school of hard knocks, Pangloss has learned nothing and his fatuous optimism remains as unshakeable as when he started out: 'after all, I am a philosopher, and it would not become me to contradict myself'. Candide, on the other hand, can see that the only way of coming to terms with a cruel, arbitrary and lawless world is to pull in one's horns and get on pragmatically with modest practical improvements. His final words in the book, addressed to the ineffable Pangloss, are: 'we must attend to our own garden' [*Il faut cultiver notre jardin*].

Rousseau could not have written those lines.[142] Satire, irony, understatement did not belong to his repertoire, for the very good reason that he himself was neither satirical nor ironic nor understated. What separated him from Voltaire and the rest of the *philosophes* – and turned him into their bitterest enemy – was not so much specific ideas as a way of doing things. This was well put by Peter Gay: 'there was something in him not to be explained by his style, his ideas, or his eccentricities alone, but compounded of all three, a strange element, that made his contemporaries uneasy'.[143] That special ingredient was Rousseau's insistence on doing everything from the inside – from inside himself. And what he found inside himself was a witches' brew of emotions, neuroses and paranoia. As his onetime friend but eventual enemy David Hume put it, Rousseau was so sensitive that it was as if he had been 'stripped not only of his clothes but of his skin'.[144] Yet this hypersensitivity was married to a wonderful talent for expressing himself in such a way as to inspire others. If Voltaire spoke to their heads, Rousseau went to their hearts, and, as Rousseau himself wrote of his mistress Madame de Warens, 'instead of listening to her heart, which gave her good counsel, she listened to her reason, which gave her bad'.[145] Fifty years later, John Keats wrote in a letter to his friend Benjamin Bailey: 'I am certain of nothing but of the holiness of the Heart's affections and the truth of the Imagination – What the imagination seizes as Beauty must be truth'.[146]

The special quality of Rousseau's achievement was brought out very well by Lytton Strachey in his *Landmarks of French Literature*, published in 1923: 'The peculiar distinction of Rousseau was his originality ... He neither represented his age, nor led it; he opposed it. His outlook upon the world was truly revolutionary ... He was a prophet, with the strange inspiration of a prophet'. At the core of his prophecy was 'his instinctive, overmastering perception of the importance and the dignity of the individual soul. It was in this perception that Rousseau's great originality lay. His revolt was a spiritual revolt ... Rousseau was the first to unite two views, to revive the medieval theory of the soul without its theological trappings, and to believe – half unconsciously, perhaps, and yet with a profound conviction – that the individual, now, on this earth, and in himself, was the most important thing in the world'.[147] The following chapter explores some of the ways in which the next generation of individuals took this insight further.

THE DARK SIDE
OF THE MOON

At the court of King Marke of Cornwall it is a clear and balmy summer's night. As the sound of hunting horns dies away, Queen Isolde eagerly awaits the arrival of her lover, Sir Tristan. Deaf to the warnings of her maid, she gives the signal that the coast is clear by extinguishing the burning torch that illuminates the entrance to her chamber. Wasting no time, the two lovers are soon clasped in a passionate embrace, pouring out their love, to the accompaniment of tumultuous music. So begins, in Act Two of Richard Wagner's *Tristan and Isolde*, one of the longest duets in all opera. In the course of twenty minutes or so (depending on the conductor), the two lovers include in their love-making an assault on the day:

> To the day! To the day!
> Our most treacherous foe,
> Let there be hatred and denunciation!

The day-time is the time of deceit, illusion, disappointment and frustration. To 'the wonder-world of the night', on the other hand, Tristan and Isolde sing a paean of praise:

> O eternal night!
> Sweet night!
> Glorious, sublime
> Night of love!

These lines initiate the final phase of the great duet, which builds to a series of grand orchestral climaxes and then ends with a piercing scream from the maid, as the cuckolded King Marke and his entourage enter. *Post coitum triste*. Tristan's reaction is: 'dreary day, for the last time!' Like Keats, Tristan and Isolde were 'half in love with easful Death'.[1]

Written between 1857 and 1859, *Tristan and Isolde* was first performed in 1865 at Munich. By this time romanticism in most branches of the creative arts was regarded as dead and buried. Only music was keeping the romantic flame burning brightly – a wholly appropriate metaphor, given the celebration of the night to be found in more than one of Wagner's music-dramas. He was the latest (but not the last) in a very long line of night worshippers. More than a hundred years earlier, in 1742, the English clergyman Edward Young started publishing a multi-part poem entitled *The Complaint, or, Night-Thoughts on Life, Death, and Immortality*. Trying to come to terms with three bereavements in quick succession, Young's poetic therapy eventually ran to around 10,000 lines of blank verse. They proved to be hugely and enduringly popular, with over a hundred collected editions published during the next fifty years.[2] The opening line – 'Tir'd nature's sweet Restorer, balmy Sleep!' – seems conventional enough, but soon Young breaks new ground by welcoming the night as the right time for exercising the imagination:

By Day the Soul is passive, all her Thoughts
Impos'd, precarious, broken, e'er mature.
By Night, from Objects free, from Passion cool,
Thoughts uncontroul'd, and unimpress'd, the Births
Of pure Election, arbitrary range.

Although Tristan and Isolde might not have agreed that the night left them 'from Passion cool', they could only have applauded Young's distaste for the 'feather'd Fopperies' beloved of daylight.

As we have seen in the previous chapter, Young struck an especially responsive chord with German intellectuals when writing about the nature of genius. And so he did with his partiality for the night. By 1759 there were ten different German translations of 'Night Thoughts' available, his admirers numbering many of the leading lights of the literary scene – Bodmer, Klopstock (who wrote an ode 'To Young'), Gellert, Wieland, Gerstenberg, Hamann, and Herder. The last-named wrote that he found the best setting for reading Young's poems a starlit summer night in a garden bordering a churchyard 'where ancient lime trees, stirred by the breath of night rustles shudders into the soul, and the philosophic owl emits from time to time its hollow accents from the ruins of a medieval castle or from its abode in the old Gothic tower'.[3] He also accorded Young the ultimate accolade by hailing him as 'a genius'.[4] Herder's friend Hamann told him he had had the uncanny experience of feeling 'as if all my hypotheses had been a mere afterbirth of [Young's] "Night Thoughts", and, as if all my whims had been impregnated with his metaphors'.[5]

This day/night duality became a favourite theme of the romantic revolution. In large measure, of course, this was a reaction to the Enlightenment's preoccupation with light as a metaphor. The frontispiece of the *Encyclopédie*, created by Charles-Nicolas Cochin, summed up the multi-volume project pictorially by depicting truth in the form of a beautiful woman surrounded by a bright light, as reason and philosophy gently remove the superstitious veils which currently hide her splendour. As Novalis complained in *Christianity, or Europe* (1799): 'Light became [the philosophers'] favourite subject on account of its mathematical obedience and freedom of movement. They were more interested in the refraction of its rays than in the play of its colours, and thus they named after it their great enterprise, Enlightenment'.[6] In that brightly lit but sterile environment, rather like a hospital ward, he observed, the poetic imagination could not hope to flourish: 'I know how like a dream all imagination is, how it loves night, meaningless, and solitude'.[7]

The visual counterpoint to Cochin's optimistic image was Henry Fuseli's painting *The Nightmare* of 1781. On a bed lies a sleeping woman, her legs apart, her arms dangling, her hair tumbling, her lips parted, her nostrils flared. On her stomach sits the goblin or incubus who is giving her such a disturbing dream. The manic mood is intensified by a mad-looking horse (the mare of the 'night-mare')[8] with bulging eyes and open mouth, thrusting its head round a red curtain. A sensation when exhibited at the Royal Academy in 1781, it also proved very popular in continental Europe, to which it spread in the form of engravings, often pirated locally.[9] Goethe's patron, Duke Karl August of Weimar, responded with enthusiasm when he saw a copy at the Leipzig book fair in 1783: 'I have not seen anything for a long time that gives me so much pleasure', he reported, and then set about collecting all available engravings by Fuseli.[10] Probably no contemporary image was so often travestied by caricaturists.

Much less well-known is the image painted by Fuseli on the back of the canvas, for the good reason that it was not revealed until the painting was acquired by the Detroit Institute of Arts in the middle of the twentieth century. This is a portrait of an attractive, shapely young woman in conventional, not to say demure pose. Although Fuseli left no record as to her identity, it is likely that it was Anna Landolt, with whom he had fallen passionately in love when on a visit to his home-town of Zürich in 1779. Aware that his lack of means ruled out marriage, he felt unable to reveal his feelings to the lady in person but had no such inhibitions when it came to pouring his heart out to his friends. To Anna's uncle, the celebrated writer Johann Kaspar Lavater, he wrote: 'Is she in Zürich now? Last night I had her in bed with me – tossed my bed-clothes huggermugger – wound my hot and tight-clasped hands about her – fused her body and her *soul* together with my own – poured into her my spirit, breath and strength. Anyone who touches her now commits adultery and incest! She is *mine*, and I am *hers*. And have her I will' and 'each earthly night since I left her, I have lain in her bed'.[11] It seems reasonable to conclude, with the art historian H.W. Janson, that the woman depicted on both sides of the canvas is Anna Landolt. On the engraved version a four-line verse by Erasmus Darwin was added:

> On his Night-Mare, thro' the evening fog,
> Flits the squab fiend, o'er fen, lake and bog,
> Seeks some love-wilder'd maid by sleep opprest,
> Alights, and grinning, sits upon her breast.[12]

If Fuseli is never mentioned today in the same breath as Reynolds or Gainsborough, he was very influential during his lifetime, both in England and on the continent, hailed as a genius by minds as diverse as Blake and Goethe.[13] Although he was so much of an individualist that he can hardly be held to be representative of anything, he did unite in one strange personality many of the forces that were eroding enlightened classicism. Ideas of restraint, balance and harmony were repugnant to him, both in his life and in his art – indeed he would make no distinction between the two. Forced to flee from Zürich at the age of twenty-one after a courageous but imprudent attack on a corrupt city magistrate, he roamed around Europe, pursuing a Bohemian life-style and acquiring the reputation revealed in his sobriquet 'the wild Swiss'. Lavater described him to Herder as:

The most original genius I know. Nothing but energy, profusion and calm! The wildness of the warrior – and the feeling of supreme sublimity! ... His spirits are storm wind, his ministers flames of fire! He goes upon the wings of the wind. His laughter is the mockery of hell and his love – a deadly lightning-flash.[14]

Herder's own assessment of Fuseli was 'a genius like a mountain torrent'.[15] Naturally, Fuseli venerated Rousseau, to the extent of writing a book about him, preceded by a frontispiece entitled 'Justice and Liberty Hanged, while Voltaire Rides Monster Humanity and Jean-Jacques Rousseau Takes his Measure'.[16] A few hours in Rousseau's company in 1776 made him 'as happy as a man can be', although he later fell out with him (in itself a very Rousseauian thing to do).[17] Naturally too, he venerated all the rough and ready rule-breaking geniuses of the past, especially Shakespeare: that is to say the Shakespeare of violence, the occult and dreams, of Macbeth's witches and Titania's erotic fantasies.[18] It was those irregular characteristics of Shakespeare which appalled the classicists that appealed to him most. As he put it in one of his aphorisms (many of which dealt with the nature of genius): 'Shakespeare is to Sophocles as the flashes of lightning of a stormy night are to daylight'.[19] The academic artists from around Europe he encountered in Rome he dismissed as 'vermin'.[20]

Fuseli went inside himself for inspiration. The brooding intensity of his many self-portraits suggests that what he found there was disturbing. The eroticism of *The Nightmare* recurs again and again, albeit often in less manic but more explicit forms. An 'erotic group' of 1809, for example, shows a recumbent male being pleasured by three naked women, the first of whom is inserting his penis into the second while the third lowers her genitalia on to his face.[21] Although it is not entirely clear whether or not the man is a willing participant, in another similar drawing, created twenty years earlier, his hands are firmly bound. Male oppression by predatory females was something of an obsession for Fuseli, the most explicit being a drawing simply entitled *Female Cruelty*, and the most memorable *Brunhild Watching Gunther Suspended from the Ceiling*. In other words, Fuseli believed that his dark fantasies were not something to be hidden, but a legitimate source of inspiration. As he himself wrote: 'dreams are one of the most unexplored regions of art'.[22]

But one man's dream can be another woman's nightmare. Not everyone cared to follow Fuseli into the darker recesses of his troubled psyche (although of course his more explicit erotica were not exhibited during his lifetime). An anonymous

Henry Fuseli, Symplegma of a Man with Three Women
(1809–10)

critic writing in the *Public Advertiser* in 1786 confessed that he
was unable to voice an opinion about the merits of Fuseli's
work: 'pictures are, or ought to be', he observed, 'a rep-
resentation of natural objects, delineated with taste and precision', whereas Fuseli 'seems to be painting everything from
fancy, which renders his work almost incomprehensible, and
leaves no criterion to judge of them by, but the imagination'.[23]
Standing in front of *The Mandrake: a Charm* at the Royal
Academy's exhibition the previous year, Horace Walpole noted
in the margin of his catalogue: 'shockingly mad, madder than
ever: quite mad'.[24] Coming from the author of *The Castle of
Otranto*, the phantasmagorian Gothic novel inspired by a bad

dream, this verdict was a classic case of the pot calling the kettle black.

In exposing his erotic side to public gaze, Fuseli was following in the footsteps of his mentor, Rousseau. In *The Confessions*, Rousseau recorded that sensuality had been 'burning in my blood' for as long he could remember. In an excited passage recalling his adolescence, he wrote of 'the restless tingling in my veins' and 'my crazy fantasies, my wild fits of eroticism', the result of being 'ardent, lascivious, and precocious by nature'. Fortunately, 'my sensibility, combined with my timidity and my romantic nature' prevented what might otherwise have been a descent 'into the most brutal sensuality'.[25] The tension between a horror of immorality and a powerful sex drive found expression not only in his auto-biography but also in his literary creations. Describing the final stages of the composition of *La nouvelle Héloïse* in 1757, he wrote: 'The return of spring had redoubled my amorous delirium, and in my erotic transports, I had composed for the last parts of *Julie* several letters that betray the ecstatic state in which I wrote them'.[26]

Such were the social pressures that few writers dared to be as frank as Rousseau. Nevertheless, the introspection that became one of romanticism's most prominent defining features ensured that sex was never far away, no matter how much it might be dressed up in a respectable vocabulary. Indeed, it might be said that romanticism was institutionally erotic. When enlightened classicism held sway, there was plenty of erotica to be found, of course – more than ever before – but these were pornographic books, often aimed at the Church, as in the case of Diderot's *La Religieuse* or the marquis d'Argens' *Thérèse Philosophe*, for example. Of quite a different order was a novel like Friedrich Schlegel's *Lucinde* of 1799, which treated sex as a path to psychological understanding rather than physical gratification. Its publication unleashed a scandal because it was well-known that it depicted the adulterous relationship between the author and Dorothea Veit, the daughter of Moses Mendelssohn, with whom he lived for some years before 'making an honest woman of her', to employ a phrase that went out of fashion only recently. Even for a reading public brought up on *Werther*, the carnality of passages such as the following account of an erotic dream by Lucinde's lover Julius was found shocking:

A subtle fire flowed in my veins; what I dreamed of wasn't just a kiss or the embrace of your arms; it wasn't just a wish to break the tormenting thorn of yearning and cool the sweet flames in surrender; I didn't yearn only for your lips or your eyes or your body. It was rather a romantic confusion of all these things, a wonderful mixture of the most various memories and yearnings ... Wit and rapture alternated between us and became the common pulse of our united life and we embraced each other with as much wantonness as religion. I begged you that for once you might give yourself completely over to frenzy, and I implored you to be insatiable.[27]

To make matters worse – *much* worse – the illicit relationship between Julius and Lucinde did not make them guilt-ridden or unhappy or lead them to a sticky end; on the contrary, it brought them joyous fulfilment. Nor did Schlegel commend himself to conventional opinion with his aphorism: 'the rights of love are higher than the ceremonies of the altar'.[28]

That the lovers embraced 'with as much wantonness as religion' shocked orthodox Christians, but did not seem a paradox to the romantics, or at least not to the Germans among them, for whom romanticism was 'the continuation of religion by aesthetic means'.[29] Those aesthetic means included an appeal to the carnal as much as to the spiritual. Indeed, the two could not be disentangled. As Schlegel's friend Clemens Brentano put it in his novel *Godwi*, only the sensuous can be truly religious, adding 'whoever has a natural inclination for sensual delight [*Wollust*] and does not indulge it, leads a truly depraved life. There is nothing more unchaste than a sensual girl who remains chaste'. Another member of the Jena group, Novalis, who habitually fused religious revelation with erotic experience, wrote that whoever touches a human body touches heaven.[30] In his 'Hymns to the Night' of 1799–1800, Novalis also provided the ultimate poetic expression of this heady mixture of darkness, death and sex.

THE WONDER-WORLD OF THE NIGHT

The night and dreams became a romantic trope. Of the many illustrations that could be found, those of Caspar David Friedrich stand out for their originality and power. The visual evidence suggests that it was mainly at night, or at least in the twilight, that his creative spirit spread its wings, as the titles of some of his most evocative paintings reveal: *Sea Piece by Moonlight*, *Seashore by Moonlight*, *Northern Sea in the Moonlight*, *Moonrise by the Sea*, *Moon above the Riesengebirge*, *Greifswald in Moonlight*, *Town at Moonrise*, *Man and Woman Contemplating the Moon*, *Two Men Contemplating the Moon*, *Two Men by the Sea at Moonrise*, *Evening on the Baltic Sea*, *The Evening Star*, not to mention the painting simply titled *Night* (which depicts a

Caspar David Friedrich, The Graveyard Gate *(1824)*

storm-tossed boat).[31] The sun does not shine often in Friedrich's paintings and, when it does, it is usually going down. Representative of his brooding, introspective œuvre is *The Grave-yard Gate* of 1824. According to a Russian visitor to his studio, Friedrich explained that it depicts the nocturnal return of a bereaved couple to the cemetery where their child had been buried earlier that day. As they peer round the gate, they see the infant spirit ascending, to be greeted by the spirits of its ancestors which hover around the other graves.[32] No knowledge of this programme is needed, however, to appreciate Friedrich's extraordinary ability to convey a sense of looking from this world into the next, just as no belief in that next world is needed to appreciate the power of his creation. When he died in 1840 at the age of sixty-five, his reputation had long been in decline and so it remained for the rest of the century. But the twentieth century witnessed his return to the pinnacle of romantic painters, as his vision took on a renewed appeal. And not just among artists: standing in front of Friedrich's *Man and Woman Contemplating the Moon* in Berlin, Samuel Beckett observed: 'This was the source of *Waiting for Godot*, you know'.[33]

The change in attitude to the night which lay at the heart of romanticism was revealed with special clarity in music. In the eighteenth century, anything titled '*notturno*' or '*Nacht-musik*' was a cheerful piece to be performed usually by wind or brass ensemble as background for an *al fresco* summer festivity. Mozart's *Eine kleine Nachtmusik* ('a little night music' or, more accurately, 'a short notturno') of 1787 is the best example in every sense, its opening bars being one of the most imme-diately recognisable pieces of music ever written, so overplayed in inappropriate surroundings – from aeroplanes to shopping malls – that it can now be heard but not listened to.

Quite a different creature was the 'nocturne' composed by John Field in 1812.[34] This was the first time that the French word had been used and the first time it had been applied to a solo piano piece. Field was an Irish expatriate, born in Dublin in 1782, who had studied in London with (and been ruthlessly exploited by) Muzio Clementi and had moved to Russia in 1802. Field combined his skills as a virtuoso pianist and intimate knowledge of the Italian operatic repertoire so popular in his adopted country to create a truly distinctive sound.[35] As any of the many recordings available reveal, this is music with an immediate, bewitching appeal. In an article written in 1859, no less a musician than Franz Liszt paid tribute: 'The name "nocturne", which Field invented, suits these pieces wonderfully well. For their opening sounds at once transport us into those nocturnal hours when the soul is liberated from mundane cares and, turned into itself alone, is elevated into those mysterious regions of the star-spangled heavens'.[36] He added that as a young man he had spent many happy hours lulled into a hallucinatory state by the 'soft intoxication' of Field's music.

Many composers were to flatter Field by imitation. In his own twenty-one nocturnes, written between 1829 and 1847, Chopin found so much depth and variety as to anchor the genre firmly in the instrument's repertoire. His Nocturne in E flat, Opus 9, no. 2, has become almost as familiar as *Eine kleine Nachtmusik*. Moreover, its main rival for pianistic ubiquity is probably Franz Liszt's Nocturne No. 3, published in 1850 and better known as 'Liebestraum'. In the course of the nineteenth century, countless other composers swelled the genre, including Schumann, Glinka, Tchaikovsky, Rimsky-Korsakov, Skryabin, Grieg, Debussy, Fauré, Satie, d'Indy and Poulenc.

The night of Field or Chopin's nocturnes is a gentle, melancholy, wistful, yearning, languorous sort of time, in short a time for romance – indeed, initially Field called the first of his nocturnes a 'romance'.[37] The pace is invariably gentle, with most of the pieces marked 'molto moderato', 'andante' or 'lento'. Even if a cloud does occasionally pass across the moon, it always seems to be spring or summer. It is music that is perfect for accompanying – or being accompanied by – the nocturnal poems so popular with the French romantics, with Alfred de Musset, for example, part of whose 'May Night' has the Muse saying:

> Poet, take up your lute; the night, above the lawn,
> Rocks the gentle breeze in its fragrant veil.
> The rose, still virgin, closes jealously
> On the pearly hornet, intoxicated as it dies.
> Listen! All is silent; think of your beloved.
> The evening, under the lime trees,
> The glow of sunset leaves a sweeter farewell in the
>   dark foliage.
> This evening, all will blossom; immortal nature
> Is filled with scents, with love and murmuring,
> Like the blissful bed of two young newlyweds.

But the night could also be a time of pain, sorrow and suffering, a time when the weather turns cold and stormy. This was how Franz Schubert saw it in 'Winter Journey', composed in the penultimate year of his short life. The twenty-four verses that make up the complete work were written by Wilhelm Müller, a Prussian poet whom Schubert never met and who died in the same year (1827). Whatever posterity may have made of the rest of his œuvre, Müller has been granted immortality by providing Schubert with the texts for his two greatest song-cycles (the other being *Die schöne Müllerin*) and deserves appropriate credit. The desperate journey his unnamed hero makes across a frozen landscape, fleeing from a love which was not just unrequited and unconsummated but also unworthy, takes place mainly at night. The linden-tree on which he had once carved tokens of his love he now passes in the dead of night. The bright flowers in warm spring sunshine he sees only in a dream when seeking refuge in a charcoal-burner's hovel. The lights he sees in the darkness turn out to be will-o'-the-wisps. As he passes through sleeping villages, the dogs bark and rattle their chains. The signposts to towns he ignores, preferring deserted tracks, for he knows that the road he has to travel leads to a place from which no one returns. Just before the end, in a song entitled 'Courage', he interrupts the unrelieved misery of his plight with a defiantly cheerful determination to go off into the world no matter what the wind and weather, for if there are no Gods to be found on earth, he exclaims, at least he himself can be one. The exaltation does not last. In the last verse he finds himself outside a village, his only company an old beggar whose bare feet and fingers are frozen and whose begging-bowl is empty.

Although Schubert was suffering a long and agonising death from syphilis, his creative powers were flourishing as never before. The thirty-odd works of his last eighteen months included the piano trios in $B^\flat$ major (D898) and $E^\flat$ major (D929), the String Quintet in C major (D956), the songs posthumously published as *Schwanengesang* (D957), three piano sonatas (D958–60) and one of his most ambitious (and greatest) songs, *Der Hirt auf dem Felsen* [The shepherd on the rock] (D965). Even in this company, the music he composed for *Winterreise* stands out for its emotional intensity. Whether sung by a tenor (Ian Bostridge), baritone (Dietrich Fischer-Dieskau) or even mezzo-soprano (Brigitte Fassbaender), the seventy-odd minutes provide the best possible musical response to Caspar David Friedrich's injunction to the artist to find what lies inside himself and then 'bring to the light of day what you have seen in the darkness, so that it can work on others, from the outside inwards'. Schubert made clear himself that Müller's poems had affected him deeply. His old friend Josef von Spaun recorded:

One day he said to me 'Come to Schober's today, I will sing you a cycle of awe-inspiring songs. I am anxious to know what you will say about them. They have affected me more than has been the case with any other songs'. So, in a voice wrought with emotion, he sang the whole of the 'Winterreise' through to us. We were quite dumbfounded by the gloomy mood of these songs and Schober said he had only liked one song 'Der Lindenbaum' [The Linden-tree]. To which Schubert only said, 'I like these songs more than all the others and you will get to like them too'; he was right, soon we were enthusiastic over the effect of these melancholy songs ... More beautiful German songs probably do not exist and they were his real swan-song.[38]

In 1815 Müller had written in his diary: 'I can neither play nor sing, yet when I write verses, I sing and play after all. If I could produce the melodies, my songs would be more pleasing than they are now. But courage! perhaps there is a kindred spirit somewhere who will hear the tunes behind the words and give them back to me'.[39]

THE SLEEP OF REASON

Field's night was soothingly warm, Schubert's night was terrifyingly cold. But what was depicted by Goya in his justly celebrated etching *El sueño de la razón produce monstros* of 1799? He presents an artist – the first of the three versions makes it clear that it is Goya himself – who has fallen asleep at his desk.[40] From behind him a flock of owls and bats fly out. One owl lands on his back, another appears to offer him a chalk-holder. At his left shoulder crouches a black cat, on the floor at the right a lynx stares at him impassively. Written on the side of the desk is the work's title. It is necessary to give the Spanish title, because '*sueño*' can mean either 'sleep' or 'dream'. This is not pedantry. The most popular reading translates it as 'The sleep of reason produces monsters' and interprets it 'not as a manifesto of a new dark art glorifying unfettered phantasy (*sic*), but as a warning which shows what happens to an artist who lets himself be overcome by his own imagination' (George Levitine).[41] Goya himself lent credence to this view of his intentions by commenting on the second version: 'The author dreaming. His only purpose is to banish harmful ideas commonly believed, and with this work of *Caprichos* to per-petuate the solid testimony of truth'. This was at a time when he intended *The Sleep of Reason* to serve as the frontispiece for the album of etchings called '*Caprichos*' [fantasies, plays of the imagination].

Further evidence of the essentially enlightened message is provided by the animals who appear. In version one there is a donkey, symbolising ignorance; a dog with his tongue hanging out, symbolising avarice; bats, symbolising hypocrisy; and a lynx, identified by a contemporary Spanish dictionary as 'one who has very keen vision and great sagacity and subtlety in understanding or in inquiring into very difficult matters'.[42] In the final version, the donkey and dog have gone, but a black cat has appeared, as a diabolic opponent of the lynx. But what

Goya, The Sleep of Reason Produces Monsters *(1799)*

of the owls? Are they the creatures associated with Athena and Minerva and hence with wisdom? Or are they '*Búhos*', associated with ignorance and the forces of darkness? So, when, in the third and final version, the owl offers Goya the chalk, is it a benign source of inspiration, encouraging him to exercise the imaginative powers released from his sub-conscious? In that case '*sueño*' would be better translated as 'dream'. Or is it an evil seducer, tempting him into the paths of madness that open up for the imagination uncontrolled by reason? In that case '*sueño*' should indeed be 'sleep'.

Goya himself did not make his intentions clear. The commentary usually ascribed to him – 'imagination forsaken by Reason begets impossible monsters; united with her, she is the mother of the arts and the source of their wonders' – was very likely written by someone else (his friend, the playwright Moratin).[43] Another plausible scenario runs as follows: Goya was undoubtedly a man of the Enlightenment. The company he chose to keep consisted in part of enlightened intellectuals – *ilustrados* – such as Gaspar Melchor de Jovellanos, their friendship immortalised in one of Goya's greatest portraits.[44] The first part of his career had been conventional – training in Saragossa, a long stay in Italy, followed on his return by patronage from the state (cartoons for the royal tapestry factory and portraits of the royal family), the Church (altar-pieces and frescoes) and aristocrats (portraits). He became a member of the Royal Academy at Madrid in 1780, its deputy director five years later and Official Painter to the King the year after that.[45]

In 1792, however, at the age of 46, Goya suffered a serious and prolonged illness that left him stone-deaf. Among other harrowing side-effects were fainting fits, spells of semi-blindness, and hallucinations.[46] When he came out the other side, his creative priorities had changed radically. As he told his friend (and vice-president of the Royal Academy) Bernardo de Iriarte, he had decided to paint a series of 'cabinet pictures' [*cuadros de gabinete*], depicting 'themes that cannot usually be dealt with in commissioned works, where *capricho* and invention do not have much of a role to play'. Six of the twelve paintings in question portrayed bullfighting, to which Goya was greatly attached, and the others feature victims of a fire at night, survivors of a shipwreck, a highway robbery, a group of strolling players, the interior of a prison, and a lunatic asylum.[47] The last-named was based on personal experience: he described it to Iriarte as 'a courtyard with lunatics, in which two naked men are fighting with their warden, who beats them and others with sacks (a scene I saw at first hand in Zaragoza)'.[48] However, the painting may well have been as much an expression of Goya's troubled state of mind as a piece of reportage.

By this time, Goya was beginning to move away from the academic context in which he had worked hitherto. In 1792, just before he fell ill, he presented to the Royal Academy his thoughts on the reorganisation of its teaching programme. Although he firmly stated his belief in the central axiom of a mimetic aesthetic, identifying the sole aim of painting as 'Nature's exact imitation', he was equally resolute in rejecting academic didacticism. 'Academies should not be restrictive', he stated. Every element of compulsion and servility must be eradicated, as must a compulsory timetable to be followed by all students, for 'there are no rules for painting'. Even the greatest artist could not explain 'how he reaches that deep understanding and appreciation of things, which is necessary for great art'. Nature must indeed be imitated but the process of imitation 'is truly a deep and impenetrable mystery!'[49]

Seven years later, when he came to write the advertisement for the *Caprichos*, he had moved still further towards an expressive aesthetic:

The author has not followed the precedents of any other artist, nor has he been able to copy Nature herself. It is very difficult to imitate Nature, and a successful imitation is worthy of admiration. He who departs entirely from Nature will surely merit high esteem, since he has to put before the eyes of the public forms and poses which have only existed previously in the darkness and confusion of an irrational mind, or one which is beset by uncontrolled passion.[50]

Although that seems unequivocal enough, Goya stressed that his primary purpose was moral improvement: 'it is as proper for painting to criticize human error and vice as for poetry and prose to do so'. His objective was to satirise 'the innumerable foibles and follies to be found in any civilized society, and ... the common prejudices and deceitful practices which custom, ignorance or self-interest have hallowed'. For good measure, he concluded the advertisement with as good a definition of art as imitation as can be imagined: 'Painting (like poetry) chooses from universals what is most apposite. It brings together in a single imaginary being, circumstances and characteristics which occur in nature in many different persons. With such an ingeniously arranged combination of properties the artist produces a faithful likeness, but also earns the title of inventor rather than that of servile copyist'.[51]

Among the eighty etchings that make up the *Caprichos*, there are certainly many which satirise contemporary targets – monks, friars, the Inquisition and the Queen's lover Manuel Godoy, for example. But as one nightmarish image follows another, whatever didactic purpose there might have been recedes into the distance. Goya has allowed his rational faculties to fall asleep and in his dreams has gone inside himself to explore his subconscious mind. What he then brings to the

Goya, All of Them Will Fall *(1799)*

surface and visualises in his own utterly unique manner justifies
all too well Alexander Pope's fears:

> With terrors round, can Reason hold her throne,
> Despise the known, nor tremble at the unknown?

Survey both worlds, intrepid and entire,
In spite of witches, devils, dreams, and fire?[52]

Goya's world is a pre-Newtonian world peopled by cripples, criminals, whores, monsters, devils, witches, magicians and lunatics, doing unspeakable things to each other. What is one to make of plate nineteen – *All of Them Will Fall*[53] – for example? In a tree sits a decoy-bird with the bust and face of a voluptuous woman. Around her flutter male birds with human faces. Their eventual fate is illustrated below, as two prostitutes and an old woman insert a stick into a plucked bird's anus, as his mouth dribbles vomit. Truly, the sleep of reason does produce monsters. Goya might well have agreed with Hamann that dreams are 'journeys to the Inferno of self-knowledge'.[54] He himself wrote that he 'drew his dreams'.[55] Around a quarter of the *Caprichos* deal with witches, an interest of Goya's that bordered on obsession. Nor does he seem to have brought to the subject the disdainful scepticism of a Voltairean *philosophe*, for he also wrote: 'as soon as day breaks, they fly each one his own way, the witches, the hobgoblins, the visions and the phantoms ... No one has ever been able to find out where they hide and lock themselves up in the daytime'.[56] In short, if Goya really was pursuing an enlightened agenda, he was doing it by means of a romantic vocabulary. As we shall see in the next chapter, experience of the armed wing of the Enlightenment, in the shape of Napoleon's armies, gave him the raw material for images just as dark and even more compelling.

In the same year that Goya published the *Caprichos* (1799), Goethe was writing the 'Walpurgis Night' episode of *Faust*. On the night before May Day, Faust and Mephistopheles make their way up the Brocken, the highest point of the Harz mountains, to attend the Witches' Sabbath. Along the way to Satan's throne, they meet creatures just as fabulous as anything that Goya imagined, among them a will-o'-the-wisp, salamanders, owls of course, trees that stretch out their roots to ensnare passers-by, witches of every shape, size and age, including 'Mother Baubo' riding on a sow, a general, a minister, a parvenu, a red mouse that jumps out of a pretty young witch's mouth when she sings, and so on. It is an episode that cried out to be turned into a film directed by the late Federico Fellini, not least in its eroticism:

> *FAUST [dancing with the young witch]*
> A pleasant dream once came to me:
> I saw a lovely apple-tree,
> And two fine apples hanging there;
> I climbed to pick that golden pair.
> *THE FAIR ONE*
> You men were always apple-mad;
> Adam in Eden was just as bad.
> I've apples in my garden too –
> How pleased I am to pleasure you!
> *MEPHISTOPHELES [with the old witch]*
> A naughty dream once came to me:
> I saw a cleft and cloven tree.
> It was a monstrous hole, for shame!
> But I like big holes just the same.
> *THE OLD WITCH*
> Greetings, Sir Cloven-Hoof, my dear!
> Such gallant knights are welcome here.
> Don't mind the outsize hole; indeed
> An outsize plug is what we need![57]

While giving free rein to his imagination, Goethe also takes the opportunity to take revenge on the doyen of the Berlin Enlightenment, Friedrich Nicolai, who had been unwise enough to publish a clumsy satire of Goethe's novel *Werther*. At the Witches' Sabbath he appears as 'Proktophantasmist', imaginatively (but appropriately) translated by David Luke as 'Mr Arsey-Phantarsey'. This grumpy old pedant is enraged that his world has been invaded by figments of Goethe's imagination:

MR ARSEY-PHANTARSEY
Damned spirit-rabble! Stop this insolence!
Hasn't it been quite clearly proved to you
You don't exist as proper people do?
....
This is outrageous! Why are you still here?
The world has been enlightened! You must disappear!
....
All my life I've tried to sweep away
This superstitious junk. It's an outrage I say![58]

THE OPIATE OF THE ARTISTS

Neither Goethe nor Goya needed artificial stimulants to release the demons from their subconsciousness. Nor did John Keats, who in *Ode on Melancholy* explicitly advised against them:

No, no, go not to Lethe, neither twist
Wolf's-bane, tight-rooted, for its poisonous vine.[59]

It was his poetic sensibility that allowed him to induce a trance-like state, as in the opening lines of *Ode to a Nightingale*:

> My heart aches, and a drowsy numbness pains
> My sense, as though of hemlock I had drunk,
> Or emptied some dull opiate to the drains
> One minute past, and Lethe-wards had sunk.[60]

Four stanzas later, he explicitly turns his back on artificial assistance:

> Away! away! for I will fly to thee,
> Not charioted by Bacchus and his pards,
> But on the viewless wings of Poesy,
> Though the dull brain perplexes and retards.[61]

Others were more inclined to take advantage of the ready availability of narcotics. They were sold over the counter without restriction, chiefly in the form of 'laudanum', an alcoholic tincture of opium. In England many household medicine-cupboards contained a bottle, to serve as a pain-killer.[62] The most candid user was Thomas De Quincey, who began taking laudanum to dull the pain of a gastric complaint, became hopelessly addicted and published his *Confessions of an English Opium Eater* in 1820. The title notwithstanding, this was less an awful warning than an account of the interior life of someone whose natural bent for introspection was intensified by the drug. De Quincey stated that his main purpose was 'to reveal something of the grandeur which belongs potentially to human dreams', including 'those trances, or profoundest reveries, which are the crown and consummation of what opium can do for human nature'.[63]

Another user, although, fortunately for him, only occasionally so, was Hector Berlioz. Among the many romantic traits he personified was intense introspection. In 1830, aged twenty-six, he wrote to his father: 'I wish I could find a specific to calm the feverish excitement which so often torments me; but I shall never find it, it comes from the way I am made. In addition, the habit I have got into of constantly observing myself means that no sensation escapes me, and reflection doubles it – I see myself in a mirror. Often I experience the most extraordinary impressions, of which nothing can give an idea; nervous exaltation is no doubt the cause, but the effect is like that of opium'.[64] He was certainly very sensitive: the mere news that his favourite Gluck opera *Iphigénie en Tauride* was going to be performed was enough to start his legs trembling, teeth chattering, head swimming and even nose bleeding.[65]

It is very likely that Berlioz was familiar with De Quincey's *Confessions* in the French version of 1828. This contains an episode added by the translator, Alfred de Musset, in which a hero under the influence of a drug imagines that he has committed a terrible crime and hears himself being sentenced to death. It thus anticipates the fourth movement of Berlioz's *Symphonie fantastique*, written in 1830 and titled 'An Episode in the Life of the Artist'.[66] His own programme note reads: 'In a fit of despair he [the artist] poisons himself with opium; but instead of killing him, the narcotic induces a horrific vision, in which he believes he has murdered the loved one, has been condemned to death, and witnesses his own execution. March to the scaffold; immense procession of headsmen, soldiers and populace. At the end the *melody* reappears once again, like a last reminder of love, interrupted by the death-stroke'.[67] Despite the emphatic sound of a falling guillotine blade, this is not the end. In the following and final movement, marked 'Dream of a witches' sabbath', the artist 'is surrounded by a hideous throng of demons and sorcerers, gathered to celebrate the sabbath night'.

The *Symphonie fantastique* has good claims to be regarded as the summit of French romanticism. Its immediate inspiration was Berlioz's unrequited passion for the Irish actress Harriet Smithson, with whom he had fallen in love when seeing her performance as Ophelia in an English-language production of *Hamlet* (of which he understood very little). It also marked his declaration of artistic independence: 'Now that I have broken the chain of routine, I see an immense territory stretching before me, which academic rules forbade me to enter'. The agent of his emancipation had been 'that awe-inspiring giant Beethoven'.[68] In a highly charged letter to his sister, he even managed to give an erotic flavour to his new departure: 'you cannot imagine what pleasure a composer feels who writes freely in response to his own will alone. When I have drawn the first accolade of my score, where my instruments are ranked in battle array, when I think of the virgin lands which academic prejudice has left untouched till now and which since my emancipation I regard as my domain, I rush forward with a kind of fury to cultivate it'.[69] Apart from Shakespeare, Musset, De Quincey, Beethoven and Goethe, the other major influences on the work read like a roll-call of the French romantics – Chateaubriand, Victor Hugo, Alfred de Vigny, and Gérard de Nerval.[70]

Berlioz's status as the supreme French romantic was also sustained by the kind of opposition he aroused from the old guard. In 1832, the *doyen* of French music critics (although Belgian by birth), François Fétis, poured scorn on Berlioz's claim that he was a revolutionary who had discovered secrets hitherto concealed to everyone else. On the contrary, Fétis wrote, he had tried to run before he could walk – and was now too old to learn better.[71] Fétis's son Édouard returned to charge two years later, asking how it was possible that such an indifferent composer should be lauded by the public as a sublime genius on a par with Beethoven and Weber? His answer was that Berlioz had been very cunning. Realising that youth was on the side of the romantics in their struggle with the classicists, he had aligned himself with the former, speaking their language and packing his work with self-consciously romantic allusions. So he was worshipped as the great original by ignoramuses who could not see that this so-called originality was nothing more than the exaggeration of long-standing musical forms and that Berlioz was incapable of developing a melodic idea beyond twenty bars.[72] A more perceptive critique of the *Symphonie fantastique* was offered by Robert Schumann, who wrote that he had gone through the score many times, 'at first bewildered, then horrified, and finally astonished and admiring'.[73]

GREAT WITS ARE SURE TO MADNESS NEAR ALLIED

Chemically assisted or not, introspective journeys to the subconscious mind could cross boundaries into realms so dark as to be no longer just individual or bizarre, or even weird, but downright mad. It was no coincidence that the turn of the century witnessed a paradigm shift in attitudes to insanity. Of course the belief that the creative mind is of necessity an odd mind goes back at least to the Greeks. This was one thing on which Plato and Aristotle could agree, opining respectively: 'in vain does one knock at the gates of poetry with a sane mind' and 'poetry demands a man with a special gift ... or a touch of madness'.[74] More recently, John Dryden had written:

> Great wits are sure to madness near allied,
> And thin partitions do their bounds divide.[75]

Yet paradoxically, the emphasis on reason engendered by the scientific revolution and the Enlightenment did not encourage a sympathetic attitude to mental abnormality. On the one hand, lunatics were no longer thought to be possessed by demons, but, on the other, they were marginalised as animals bereft of man's most precious asset: his rational faculty. Even as revisionist a historian as Roy Porter, at pains to rescue the age of the Enlightenment from its image as a 'dark age' for the insane, has to concede that: 'those horror stories of lunatics chained in underground dungeons in France, whipped in Germany, and jeered by ogling sightseers in London's Bedlam – all are true. Manacled, naked, foul, sleeping on straw in overcrowded and feculent conditions, the mad were dehumanised'.[76]

Porter also recognised that 'the romantic movement renewed interest in the mad genius that had been cultivated by Renaissance Platonism but dampened by the age of reason'.[77] In their different ways, Goethe's suicidal Werther, Wordsworth's 'Idiot Boy', Southey's 'Idiot', Blake's Nebuchadnezzar, Fuseli's 'Crazy Kate', Byron's 'Lament of Tasso', Delacroix's *Portrait of Tasso* – and the many other depictions of dementia with which the period abounded – testified to the appeal of madness. Introspection, combined with a belief in the paramountcy of the individual, prompted many romantics not just to take an interest in insanity but also to be sympathetic to those afflicted. The disturbing visions inside their own psyches drew both Fuseli and Goya to depictions of asylums, for example 'drawn from memory after a real scene in the Hospital of S. Spirito at Rome' and 'The Madhouse at Saragossa' respectively.[78] A particularly eloquent contrast is provided by the Bedlam scene from Hogarth's *The Rake's Progress* of 1735 and Théodore Géricault's five studies of deranged people almost a century later. The former displays Tom Rakewell in the process of being manacled, as around him cavort such stock types as the religious fanatic, the mad mathematician, the mad musician and the naked man who thinks he is king, as curious members of the public look on. Géricault, on the other hand, was commissioned to paint the portraits by Dr Etienne-Jean Georget, one of the pioneers of psychiatric care at the Salpetrière in Paris. The results were as far removed from Hogarth's freak-show as could be imagined, but all the more disturbing.[79]

For some romantics, compassionate understanding could even be elevated into something approaching respect or even envy. The insane, they believed, had found a way of getting back to a Rousseauian state of nature by liberating themselves from a repressive civilisation that dictated normality. As the creations of Cowper, Hölderlin, Clare, Blake, Kleist, Dadd, Smart, Brentano or Schumann suggested, access to mystical insights into higher forms of truth awaited those who could let their spirits range uninhibited by social constraints.[80] William Blake wrote in the margin of his copy of J.G. Spurzheim's

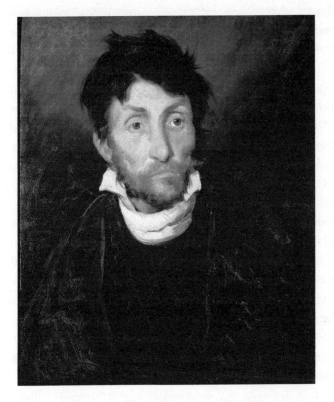

Théodore Gericault, Kleptomania (c. *1822*)

Observations on the Deranged Manifestations of the Mind, or Insanity (1817): 'Cowper came to me and said: "O that I were insane always. I will never rest. Can you not make me truly insane? I will never rest until I am so. O that in the bosom of God I was hid. You retain health and yet are as mad as any of us all – over all of us – mad as a refuge from unbelief – from

Bacon, Newton and Locke".[81] Those who found their way back to what passed for normality sometimes looked back on their delirium with nostalgia – Charles Lamb, for example, who told his friend Coleridge: 'I look back on it at times with a gloomy kind of Envy. For while it lasted I had many hours of pure happiness. Dream not, Coleridge, of having tasted all the grandeur and wildness of Fancy, till you have gone mad. All now seems to me vapid; comparatively so'.[82] Gérard de Nerval was more terse: 'I do not know why they call it illness – I never felt better'.[83]

Of all the romantic depictions of madness, the most popular and enduring were those delivered on the operatic stage, not least because they combined the visual and the poetic with the musical. As Ellen Rosand has observed: 'If madness is a peculiarly operatic condition because it licenses the suspension of verisimilitude, so opera itself can be said to be generically mad, for its double language provides a perfect model for the splitting or fragmentation of character'.[84] Although not unknown in the past – both Monteverdi and Cavalli had composed operas with mad scenes – there was a veritable flood of them during the first half of the nineteenth century: in Bellini's *Il Pirata*, *La Sonnambula* and *I Puritani*; Donizetti's *Anna Bolena*, *Lucia di Lammermoor*, *Torquato Tasso*, *Maria Padilla* and *Linda di Chamonix*; Verdi's *Nabucco* and *Macbeth*; Meyerbeer's *L'Étoile du Nord* and *Dinorah*, and Thomas's *Hamlet*, just to mention the more celebrated.[85] They were also among the most popular, reaching a genuinely mass audience right across Europe, as Italian romantic operas swept the board during the middle decades of the nineteenth century. The best of them, moreover, have never been out of the repertoire since, indeed have never been so accessible as they are today. Thanks to technological advances, it is possible to experience, for example, Joan Sutherland's classic performance of the mad scene in Act III of Donizetti's *Lucia di Lammermoor* at the Metropolitan Opera House, New York, in 1982 – and also the ecstatic response of the audience, whose cheering, shouting and stamping brought the performance to a standstill for several minutes.[86]

In depicting Lucia's collapse into homicidal insanity, Donizetti was able to draw on his own experiences. By the time he came to compose the music in 1835 he had been suffering from the terrible symptoms of syphilis for many years, though it did not kill him until 1848. As two specialists who have examined his medical history conclude, he was able to portray 'in musical, physical, psychological, biological and dramatic terms the devastating effects of psychosis on a human being'.[87] Unhappily, he was not alone in suffering from this terrible disease. Among other musicians to be afflicted were Schubert, Paganini, Schumann, Hugo Wolf and Frederick Delius.

Madness was sung, madness was acted, and madness was also danced, most influentially in *Giselle*, first performed in Paris in 1841. With a libretto by Jules-Henri Vernoy marquis de Saint-Georges and Théophile Gautier based on a poem by Heinrich Heine, music by Adolphe Adam, and choreography by Jean Coralli and Jules Perrot, it can claim to be the archetypal romantic ballet. Set in the Rhineland, it tells the story of a peasant girl who goes mad and dies when she discovers that her lover is an aristocrat in disguise already betrothed to a princess. In the second Act she returns from the dead to redeem her faithless lover by her loving forgiveness. Of all the performing arts, it was ballet that was most durably affected by the changes brought by romanticism. As Marion Kant has written: 'romanticism gave dance its particular and enduring look'.[88]

Introspection took the romantics to some of the darker recesses of the human psyche. It also led them to populate their creations with very different kinds of heroes and heroines. Among the many fictional representatives of the Enlightenment available, perhaps the most appropriate choice would be Robinson Crusoe, on account of his immense and enduring popularity. Born into the 'middle state' of society which, his father told him, was the best place to be in terms of happiness, Crusoe embarked on a career in commerce. Establishing himself as a merchant in Brazil he used the 400% profit he realised on his first consignment of English goods to buy a black slave and to hire a white servant. Shipwrecked on his desert island, Crusoe at once set about making the best of it: 'as reason is the substance and original of mathematics, so by stating and squaring every thing by reason, and by making the most rational judgment of things, every man may be in time master of every mechanick art'. He soon found himself neglecting worship on Sundays for the good reason that he lost count of the days. When he found barley suddenly starting to grow, he believed a miracle had occurred and turned to God – but rather lost his enthusiasm on discovering that it came from the chicken-feed he had thrown out. Although his first instinct on discovering cannibals was to kill them, more mature reflection prompted him 'to leave them to the justice of God, who is the governour of nations, and knows how by national

96

punishments to make a just retribution for national offences'. Man Friday he converted to Protestant Christianity but without coercion; Friday's father was allowed to go on worshipping his pagan Gods; and a Spaniard whom they liberated was allowed to remain a Catholic. Crusoe concluded proudly: 'I allowed liberty of conscience throughout my dominions'.

No wonder this enterprising, rational, tolerant, well-balanced man survived to return home to England and live happily ever after. His world was very far removed from that of the two archetypal heroes created by Goethe in 1773–4. The first appeared in the eponymous drama *Götz von Berlichingen with the Iron Hand*. Set at the time of the Lutheran Reformation, it chronicles the decline and fall of a knight for whom the times are seriously out of joint. Confronted by ambitious princes, greedy townspeople and revolting peasants, not to mention a scheming *femme fatale*, his virtues of honesty, integrity and loyalty prove hopelessly inadequate. As he laments to his wife, they live in degenerate times when the rule of deceit has begun. Outmanoeuvred and then betrayed, he dies gasping the word 'Liberty!'[89]

Liberty is the drama's central theme. In the most important single line of the play, the anti-hero Adelbert von Weislingen proclaims: 'One thing is for certain: happy and great alone is the man who needs neither to command nor to obey to amount to something!'[90] Any kind of authority which was not self-generated but was imposed from outside was to be rejected. Rules were out. For this reason, if no other, Goethe turned his back on classical drama with demonstrative radicalism. The unities of time, place, and action – the defining features of the dominant French model – were not so much abandoned as turned on their head. The action sprawls over several months, there are dozens of scene changes, and there are at least two main plots. The reaction of contemporaries brought up in the classical tradition was outraged. In a pamphlet entitled *Concerning German Literature; the faults of which it can be accused; the causes of the same and the means of rectifying them*, Frederick the Great derided *Götz* as 'an abominable imitation of those bad English plays', by which he meant the 'ludicrous farces' of Shakespeare.[91]

A year later, in 1774, Goethe created another and very different kind of hero in *The Sufferings of Young Werther*. Already the leading German poet and playwright of his generation, he now added the novel to the genres he had conquered. With its contemporary setting and epistolary form, *Werther* had all the apparent immediacy and spontaneity of a private correspondence. Into that realist frame, however, Goethe placed a hero whose morbid hypersensitivity could only find release in language of intense passion. Only about 40,000 words long, it packed an intense punch. The plot is quickly recounted: Werther, a young man of middle class but respectable station, meets and falls in love with Lotte, who returns his feelings but has already committed herself to another. Unable to come to terms with his frustrated passion, Werther shoots himself.

The Sufferings of Young Werther evoked a response like few novels before or since. The challenge it thrust in the face of cultural convention was so fierce that indifference was impossible. On the right, clerical conservatives found its glamorisation of suicide repugnant; on the left, enlightened progressives found its disparagement of reason equally offensive.[92] But the book's admirers drowned the criticism with paeans of emotional praise worthy of Werther himself. The poet, critic and journalist Christian Daniel Schubart told his readers: 'Here I sit, my heart melting, my breast pounding, my eyes weeping tears of ecstatic pain, and do I need to tell you, dear reader, that I have been reading *The Sufferings of Young Werther* by my beloved Goethe? Or should I rather say that I have been devouring it?'[93] Within a year there were eleven editions in print, most of them pirated; by 1790 there were thirty. Quickly translated into French and English, by the end of the century it was available in almost every European language.[94] The novel also created a market for Werther memorabilia such as images, clothes and all kinds of artefacts, which entrepreneurs were quick to supply. Top of the range were the exquisite dinner services and other china items decorated with characters and scenes from the novel produced by the Royal Saxon porcelain works at Meissen.[95]

Goethe's two types of hero – the anarchic man of action and the melancholy, hypersensitive intellectual – were to recur again and again in every genre. And so was a third kind of hero – the creator himself. In Nick Dear's play for television *Eroica*, first transmitted by the BBC in 2003, the first rehearsal of Beethoven's third symphony in the Lobkowitz Palace in Vienna in 1804 is depicted. Half-way through, the aged Joseph Haydn appears. At the end, he is asked for his opinion of the work and replies: 'very long, very tiring', to which Princess Lobkowitz objects, 'Unusual though, wasn't it?' Haydn agrees, adding: 'Unusual – he's done something no other composer has attempted. He's placed himself at the centre of his work. He's given us a glimpse into his soul – I expect that's why it's so noisy. But it is quite, quite new – the artist as hero – quite new. Everything is different from today'.[96]

This is fictional but it is not wrong. Beethoven did make

himself the hero of his works, by taking the expressive aesthetic to a new level. In 1802, the year before he began composition of the *Eroica*, he had written a will, leaving everything to his two brothers. This was not a legal document but an impassioned *cri de cœur*, railing against the cruel stroke of fate that was depriving him of his hearing. Only his art, he wrote, and the need to express everything that was inside him, had restrained him from taking his own life. He ended with the anguished plea: 'Oh Providence, vouchsafe me at least one single day to me – When, oh when, oh Divine Godhead – shall I once feel it in the Temple of Nature and among mankind? Never? No, that would be too hard'.[97] Discovered among his papers after his death and promptly published, this 'Heiligenstadt Testament', named after the village outside Vienna where he had written it, became one of the seminal documents of romanticism. Beethoven both personified and advanced the romantic revolution. He succeeded in combining both types of Goethe's hero – both Götz and Werther dwelt within his breast. In music he was the true mould-breaker, establishing the model of the composer as the angry, unhappy, original, uncompromising genius, standing above ordinary mortals and with a direct line to the Almighty. Already during his lifetime a flood of anecdotes was in circulation in the public prints, projecting 'the composite picture of the archetype martyr to art, the new kind of secular saint who was taking over from the old Christian calendars as a focus of public veneration'.[98]

It was not just the revolutionary originality of his music and his phenomenal pianistic skills that forced contemporaries to view Beethoven as so much more than a musician. It was also his behaviour, his way of life, his clothes, even – one might almost say especially – his appearance. The number of people who actually experienced Beethoven at first hand was very small, but his image was broadcast far and wide. He was the first musician to become the centre of a cult, a legend in his own lifetime. In the year that Beethoven died, the fourteen-year-old Richard Wagner heard one of his symphonies (the seventh) for the first time and was bowled over. But what threw him into a characteristically Wagnerian frenzy of enthusiasm was not just the sounds he heard in the Leipzig Gewandhaus, there was also 'the added impact of Beethoven's physiognomy, as shown by lithographs of the time, as well as the knowledge of his deafness and his solitary and withdrawn life. There soon arose in me an image of the highest supernal originality, beyond comparison with anything'.[99]

In his review of Beethoven's Fifth Symphony, published in two instalments in the *General Musical Review* of Leipzig in 1810, E.T.A. Hoffmann, himself a gifted composer, wrote:

Beethoven's music sets in motion the machinery of awe, of fear, of terror, of pain, and awakens that infinite yearning which is the essence of romanticism. Beethoven is a purely romantic, and therefore truly musical, composer. Beethoven bears the romanticism of music which he expresses with such originality and authority in his works, in the depths of his spirit. The reviewer has never felt this more acutely than in the present symphony. It unfolds Beethoven's romanticism, rising in a climax right to the end, more than any other of his works, and irresistibly sweeps the listener into the wonderful spirit-realm of the infinite.[100]

In a later essay on Beethoven's instrumental music, Hoffmann offered a more general observation that became his most celebrated aphorism: 'music is the most romantic of all the arts, one might almost say the only one that is genuinely romantic, since its only subject-matter is infinity'.[101] With all the other arts, the mediation of the intellect was required for perception; music alone could gain immediate entry to the psyche: 'music reveals to man an unknown realm, a world quite separate from the outer sensual world surrounding him, a world in which he leaves behind all feelings circumscribed by intellect in order to embrace the inexpressible'.[102]

In short, Beethoven was the perfect hero for his time. Born in 1770, he reached maturity just as the French Revolution was turning the world upside down. Like his almost exact contemporary, Napoleon Bonaparte (born in 1769), he tore up the rule-book and proved by example that careers really could be open to talents. Both men demonstrated that, while the Revolution had failed to establish the reign of liberty, it did create a culture in which charisma was at a premium. In the recent past, the words 'charisma' and 'charismatic' have been so debased by over-usage and careless application to any public figure that catches media attention as to become little more than synonyms for 'glamour' and 'glamorous'. It is therefore necessary to remind ourselves that originally it meant simply 'gift from God'. Its emergence as the crucial legitimator in politics and culture was a development of long standing, deriving from the inexorable expansion of the public sphere during the past century or so, but it was only after 1789 that it was able to thrust aside such rival claimants as tradition and contract. With the old regime being shaken until its teeth rattled, politics and culture combined to create a space in which genius could flourish as never before.[103]

This comparison between emperor and musician is less

fanciful than it might sound, if only because it was often made by contemporaries. Nor was it confined to Beethoven. In 1824 Stendhal published his *Life of Rossini*, which begins: 'Napoleon is dead; but a new conqueror has already shown himself to the world; and from Moscow to Naples, from London to Vienna, from Paris to Calcutta, his name is constantly on every tongue. The fame of this hero knows no bounds save those of civilisation itself; and he is not yet thirty-two! The task which I have set myself is to trace the paths and circumstances which have carried him at so early an age to such a throne of glory'.[104] This was no exaggeration. Right across Europe after 1815, Rossini bestrode the musical scene like a colossus. His stupendous success was the clearest possible sign that the musical public sphere had come of age. Lord Byron, whose own charismatic appeal rivalled Rossini's, wrote in 1819: 'There has been a splendid opera lately at San Benedetto – by Rossini – who came in person to play the harpsichord – the people followed him about – crowned him – cut off his hair "for memory" – he was shouted for and sonnetted and feasted – and immortalised much more than either of the emperors'.[105]

Rossini could reach his audience only at one remove, through the medium of the opera singers who drew off their own share of the applause. The musician who showed the way to a direct relationship with the public was his fellow-countryman and near-contemporary Niccolò Paganini (1782–1840). It was he who showed what a musician blessed with charisma could achieve. It was not just his technical skill, although everyone agreed that it was phenomenal. He also attracted – and carefully cultivated – an aura of mystery, danger, even diabolism. That his career had only taken off so late was thought to be especially suggestive. It was rumoured that he had perfected his technique while serving twenty years in prison for murdering his mistress, indeed that his G-string was made from a section of her intestine.[106] Others went further: no one could play so well without supernatural assistance, it was maintained, so it was variously reported that Paganini had captured the Devil in his sound-box or that he had made a Faustian pact with the Devil, sacrificing his soul in return for matchless skill. It was further alleged that he never allowed anyone to see him without footwear, lest his cloven hoof should become visible. In Vienna, some members of the audience claimed to have seen the Devil directing his bow, thus allowing him to play at superhuman speed.[107] The link with Napoleon was also often made. For example, a member of the orchestra performing his second violin concerto in Paris wrote on the score:

> In our present century nature wished
> To demonstrate her infinite power;
> To amaze the world she created two men:
> Bonaparte and Paganini![108]

Paganini blazed across the musical sky in a career that was as intense as it was brief, his burnt-out shell quickly falling back to earth. But long before he died in 1840, a far brighter and much more durable star had risen. This was Franz Liszt, as phenomenally gifted a pianist as Paganini was a violinist. In 1834 Mendelssohn came away from Erard's piano showroom in Paris shaking his head and proclaiming that he had just witnessed a miracle, for his fiendishly demanding new piano concerto had just been played sight unseen by Liszt with great brilliance and without error.[109] As with Paganini, flawless technique was only the start. Liszt also had the ability to inspire in his listeners the belief that he was superhuman, with the capacity to transport them to a level of aesthetic experience previously undreamt of. From the rich repertoire of comments on his charisma, the following, from Hans Christian Andersen, must suffice: 'When Liszt entered the saloon, it was as if an electric shock passed through it ... The whole of Liszt's exterior and movements reveal one of those persons we remark for their peculiarities alone; the Divine hand has placed a mark on them which makes them observable among thousands'.[110]

The fame he achieved was commensurate, far greater than anything enjoyed by any previous creative artist. Wherever Liszt went – and his tours took him all over Europe, from Galway to Ukraine – the crowned heads and their courtiers clamoured to meet him, to flatter him, and to give him decorations. When he left Berlin in 1842 he did so in a carriage pulled by six white horses, accompanied by a procession of thirty other coaches and an honour-guard of students, as King Frederick William IV and his Queen waved goodbye from the royal palace. As the music critic Ludwig Rellstab put it, he left 'not *like* a king, but *as* a king'.[111] Perhaps Liszt's greatest achievement was to complete the transition of musician from servant to master. This was very well put by his biographer, Alan Walker, when he wrote: 'Beethoven, by dint of his unique genius and his uncompromising nature, had forced the Viennese aristocracy at least to regard him as their equal. But it was left to Liszt to foster the view that an artist is a superior being, because divinely gifted, and the rest of mankind, of whatever social class, owed him respect and even homage'.[112]

As with Paganini, part and parcel of his charisma was his sex appeal. An important part of his titanic image was his well-deserved reputation as a lady-killer, with a preference for the ladies of the highest society. Among his early conquests was the Countess Adèle Laprunarède, who later became the duchesse de Fleury, and Countess Pauline Plater. When the latter was asked to rank the three great pianists who had performed in her salon – Hiller, Chopin and Liszt – she replied that Hiller would make the best friend, Chopin the best husband, and Liszt the best lover. The relative merits of their piano-playing do not seem to have been her main concern.[113]

Perhaps the only contemporary who could compete with Liszt in terms of charisma was Byron, for whom Liszt himself entertained 'an unbelievable passion'.[114] Unlike Byron, Liszt was exclusively (and very actively) heterosexual, but that did not prevent him from enthusing again and again about his 'beautiful and lasting passion' for the poet.[115] The comment of Lady Blessington to Liszt that '[You] resemble Bonaparte and Lord Byron!!!' sent him into a paroxysm of delight.[116] Byron would also have been thrilled by such a compliment, for his own identification with Napoleon was both intense and long-lasting. Even as a schoolboy at Harrow, he had treasured a bust of his hero, defiantly disregarding the war that was currently raging.[117] The reverse association was often made. In 1831, seven years after the death of Byron and ten years after the death of Napoleon, Macaulay wrote: 'two men have died within our recollection, who at a time of life at which few people have completed their education, had raised themselves, each in his own department, to the height of glory. One of them died at Longwood, the other at Missolonghi'.[118] Napoleon and Beethoven – Napoleon and Rossini – Napoleon and Paganini – Napoleon and Liszt – Napoleon and Byron – one contemporary after another made the identification between military conqueror and cultural hero. The French Revolution had cleared the way for the former, the romantic revolution for the latter.

The adulation lavished on these heroes revealed that the dual revolution had given rise to a new kind of relationship with their public. Their earlier equivalents had had admirers, but they had fans – not for nothing does the word derive from 'fanatic'. Also significant was the growing importance of sex appeal. The women (and sometimes men too) who threw themselves at Paganini, Liszt and Byron were demonstrating that, in the public sphere, an intimate relationship between artist and audience – however virtual it might be – was both possible and necessary. It was encouraged by the technological advances that facilitated the reproduction of images, especially the invention of lithography by the Bavarian Alois Senefelder in 1796. No one seems to have cared much what Mozart looked like, but every music lover wanted a picture of Beethoven, the first musician to become a cult, a legend in his own lifetime.

The generation of mass enthusiasm could also open the way to a wider sphere of influence. Although Beethoven confined his strongly held opinions to the private sphere, many other romantic heroes used their charismatic appeal to address the public on topical issues. With this, we move from the interior world of the individual artist to the exterior dimension of social and political change, which will be the subject of the next chapter.

3

LANGUAGE, HISTORY AND MYTH

Towards the end of the last letter he writes to his beloved Lotte before shooting himself, Goethe's Werther begins to lapse into incoherence in a delirious passage which begins: 'I am not dreaming, I am in no delusion! When nearing the grave my inner light increases.'[1] Always out of joint with the world he had to endure, poor Werther had sought comfort in introspection. As he put it in one of his first letters to his friend Wilhelm: 'I return into myself and find a world!'. Alas, his interior world proved to be a lonely place – 'a world of groping and vague desires rather than one of clear delineation and active force'.[2] His predicament was shared by many romantics. Peeling away layer upon layer of inherited rules and traditions both emancipated and isolated the artist. The pure ego was free but frail.

Caspar David Friedrich was not the only introverted genius to succumb to depression and to attempt suicide.[3] One who succeeded in taking his own life was the poet Thomas Chatterton (1752–70), whose untimely end (he was only seventeen) was mythologised by, among others, Coleridge, Shelley, Wordsworth (who called him 'the marvellous boy, the sleepless soul that perished in his pride') and Dante Gabriel

Rossetti. John Keats dedicated *Endymion* (1818) to him and also wrote an Ode in his honour:

> O CHATTERTON! how very sad thy fate!
> Dear child of sorrow – son of misery!
> How soon the film of death obscur'd that eye,
> Whence Genius mildly flash'd, and high debate.

His posthumous fame as a romantic *avant la lettre* also crossed the Channel. Alfred de Vigny's drama *Chatterton* (1835) contrasted the sensitive, aesthete hero with the brutally philistine materialists John Bell, a manufacturer, and Lord Beckford, a merchant prince. As if the suicide of a young poet in a garret were not romantic enough, Vigny invented a relationship between Chatterton and Mrs Bell, thus allowing him to end the play with a *Liebestod* as the two expired together. Rarely performed today, it nevertheless has good claims to be regarded as 'the most intelligent and, in the opinion of many critics, the finest work of the French Romantic theatre'.[4]

Rescue from isolation could be achieved by connecting the self to a greater entity, with the nation in pole position for most romantics. Two years before he wrote *The Sufferings of Young Werther*, Goethe had pointed the way in his essay 'Concerning German Architecture' inspired by the cathedral at Strassburg. It was there that he had his 'German experience' in March 1770 at the age of twenty-one.[5] No place could have been better suited to awaken his sense of nationality. A former Free Imperial City and early centre of the Lutheran Reformation, it had been seized by Louis XIV in 1681 and formally incorporated into France at the Treaty of Ryswick in 1697. So it was on German-speaking but French-ruled soil

Henry Wallis, The Death of Chatterton *(1858)*

that Goethe experienced a cultural conversion-experience. In his autobiography *Poetry and Truth*, published in 1811, he recalled his enthusiastic response to this Gothic masterpiece which he also claimed for Germany.[6]

The essay in which Goethe had proclaimed his conversion was published in 1773 in a collection entitled *On the German Character and German Art* [*Von deutscher Art und Kunst*] edited by his friend Johann Gottfried Herder, whom he had first met three years earlier. This slim volume has been hailed as 'the manifesto or charter of the *Sturm und Drang*, indeed one might go further than this and claim it as the true starting point of the German Romantic movement'.[7] In fact, as good a case could be made for Herder's treatise *On the Origin of Language*, written in 1770 but not published until 1772, for it was his emphasis on the importance of language that was to be at the heart of the cultural and political revolution that followed. Or rather one should say: the importance of each specific national language. For human beings, Herder argued, the vital link between part and whole, between one individual and another, between individual and community, between humans and the natural world, is language, the most important single concept in his intellectual system. Without language there can be no knowledge, no self-consciousness, no awareness of others, no social existence, no history. Language was not the direct creation of God, there had been no Tower of Babel. Nor was it the invention of human reason, rather its precondition, both the most natural and most necessary human function. The earliest language derived from the senses and even when abstractions and concepts emerged, they were underpinned by sensual impressions and reactions.[8] Of all the conditions and forces that underpinned a community, language was the most fundamental: 'each nation speaks in the manner it thinks and thinks in the manner it speaks ... We cannot think without words'.[9]

Language was also the force which created what Herder saw as the fundamental unit of human existence – the *Volk*. Of all German words difficult to translate into English, this is one of the most intractable. 'People' seems the most obvious choice, but *Volk* means much more than just an aggregate of individuals (for which the German equivalent is *Leute*). It also denotes a community bound by ethnic and cultural ties, as in 'the German people', together with a populist implication, as in 'the common people'. For that reason, the Oxford-Duden German Dictionary offers 'nation' as one possible translation of *Volk*. The *Volk* constitutes the nation, while the nation is of the people (*völkisch*). In the *Volk*'s language are expressed all the environmental conditions in which it developed: 'climate, water and air, food and drink, they all affect language ... Viewed in this way, language is indeed a magnificent treasure store, a collection of thoughts and activities of the mind of the most diverse nature'.[10] It was also a character that was unique, for 'every language bears the stamp of the mind and character of a national group'.[11]

This populist view of language was to have a long and influential history. For example, in his 'Advertisement' for his enormously successful novel *The Antiquary*, published in 1816, Walter Scott wrote that he had chosen his principal characters from the common people, because:

I agree with my friend Wordsworth, that they seldom fail to express themselves in the strongest and most powerful language. This is, I think, peculiarly the case with the peasantry of my own country, a class with whom I have long been familiar. The antique force and simplicity of their language, often tinctured with the Oriental eloquence of Scripture, in the mouths of those of an elevated understanding, give pathos to their grief, and dignity to their resentment.[12]

Indeed, Scott was the first significant novelist to make any attempt to use the vernacular.[13]

Binding together individual and group was the notion of self-determination. Summing up both the aesthetics and ethics of *Sturm und Drang*, Herder wrote to his fiancée Caroline Flachsland in 1773: 'All our actions should be self-determined, in accordance with our innermost character – we must be true to ourselves'.[14] And so should nations: 'the best culture of a nationality ... cannot be forced by a foreign language. It thrives only on the native soil of nationality and in the language which the nationality inherited and which continues to transmit itself'.[15] Being true to oneself meant being true to one's nation, and vice versa. Introspective subjectivism did not need to result in the sort of existential loneliness that afflicted Werther but could and should lead to a creative life within the national community.

Herder was a cultural pluralist, firmly believing that every culture had its own value, a value moreover to be understood on its own terms, from the inside out, and not judged according to some allegedly objective scale of values.[16] To paraphrase Ranke's celebrated dictum about every age, every culture for Herder was immediate to God. That did not inhibit him from advancing the special claims of his own language to be especially 'original', closest to the ancient Greeks and 'more perfect for philosophy than any other of the living languages'.[17] In part, this pride can be explained by his hostility to the triumphalism of French-speakers. In the course of the long reign of Louis XIV (1643–1715), a combination of military power and cultural imperialism propelled French from just one of several competing languages to the acknowledged medium for civilised discourse throughout Europe. A symbolic moment came in the year before the Sun King's death, when for the first time a Holy Roman Emperor (Charles VI) agreed to sign an international treaty (Rastadt) drafted in French rather than Latin.[18] The marquis de Dangeau boasted to the Académie française: 'all our works contribute to the embellishment of our language and help to make it known to foreigners. The wonders achieved by the King have made the French language as familiar to our neighbours as their own vernacular, indeed the events of these past few years have broadcast it over all the oceans of the globe, making it as essential to the New World as to the Old'.[19]

Along with the French language went French culture in all its various forms. In 1689 an anonymous German writer had lamented his compatriots' obsession with 'French language, French clothes, French food, French furniture, French dances, French music, the French pox . . . perhaps there is also a French death! Hardly have the children emerged from their mothers' wombs than people think of giving them a French teacher . . . To please the girls, even if one is ugly and deformed, one must wear French clothes'.[20] This trend accelerated during the next half-century or so. Frederick the Great of Prussia, a Franco-phone Francophile who used the German language only to shout at his soldiers, abuse his servants and instruct his officials, recorded that every German with social pretensions felt obliged to travel to Versailles and ape French fashions: 'French taste has ruled our kitchens, our furniture, our clothes and all those knick-knacks which are so at the mercy of the tyranny of fashion. Carried to excess, this passion degenerated into a frenzy; women, who are often prey to exaggeration, pushed it to the point of extravagance'.[21]

This kind of modish imitation was as far removed from individual and national self-determination as it was possible to imagine and provoked furious denunciations from Herder. In 1768, when only twenty-five, a journey to France had turned him into a Francophobe nationalist. From Nantes, where he spent several months, he wrote to his friend and mentor Hamann: 'I am now in Nantes where I am getting to know the French language, French habits and the French way of thinking – getting to know but not getting to embrace, for the closer my acquaintance with them is, the greater my sense of alienation becomes'.[22] Paris he detested as a place 'festooned with luxury, vanity and French nothingness', a decadent den of vice.[23] In a poem 'To the Germans' he appealed to his fellow-countrymen:

> Look at other nationalities! Do they wander about
> So that nowhere in the whole world they are strangers
> Except to themselves?
> They regard foreign countries with proud disdain.
> And you German, returning from abroad,
> Would you greet your mother in French?
> O spew it out before your door,
> Spew out the ugly slime of the Seine.
> Speak German, O you German![24]

Foreign travel never did anything to broaden Herder's sympathy for other nations: during a visit to Italy in 1788–9 he wrote home that the more he got to know the local people and their ways, the more enthusiasm he felt for the Germans.[25]

Herder was not alone in his wish to promote the German language. Societies for that purpose had existed since the seventeenth century. They were given fresh impetus in the late eighteenth century by a surge of cultural achievement, especially in music (the Bachs, Haydn, Mozart), philosophy (Kant, Herder, Fichte) and literature (Klopstock, Goethe, Schiller). As pride inflated, so did sensitivity to what was thought to be disparagement on the part of foreigners, especially the French. Voltaire's merciless satire on the quintessentially clod-hopping German in the person of Baron Thunder-ten-Tronck in his best-seller *Candide* was only the most successful of many such satires. In his *French and German Letters* of 1740 the Provençal Éléazar de Mauvillon, who had spent most of his adult life in Germany, depicted the Germans as being exceedingly avaricious, addicted to alcohol, brutal towards their poor, pedantic, stupid, with strong bodies but feeble minds. Their food was inedible, he added, and their wine undrinkable. At the root of the problem, he maintained, was their dreadful language: 'the difficulty that all nations have in understanding German provides good evidence of the country's barbarism. I know Frenchmen who have lived there for forty years and don't know two words of the language'. Is it their fault or the fault of a language which sounds ugly and has a clumsy grammar and syntax? he asked rhetorically. No wonder that even the best German writers were pedantic and devoid of wit.[26] 'Our language has become the language of Europe' asserted a French musical periodical in 1773, while Antoine de Rivarol proclaimed that one could now speak of 'the French world' in the same way that once one could speak of 'the Roman world'. Mankind now formed a single republic, he added, under the domination of one language.[27]

Then as now, advocates of the French language stressed its clarity, thus making it the perfect medium for the expression of enlightened truths. Diderot, for example, boasted: 'French is made to instruct, enlighten, and convince; Greek, Latin, Italian and English to persuade, move and deceive. Speak Greek, Latin, or Italian to the people, but speak French to the wise'.[28] German he did not even mention. This linguistic patriotism was only enhanced by the French Revolution and the ideological and military power it unleashed. Bertrand de Barère told the National Convention in January 1794 that French was 'the most beautiful language of Europe, the first to have consecrated the rights of man and the citizen, and the language which is charged with the role of transmitting to the world the most sublime thoughts of liberty and the greatest political speculations'.[29] Significantly, he went on, the minority languages spoken in the French Republic were ideologically suspect: 'federalism and superstition speak Breton; emigration and hatred of the Republic speak German; counter-revolution speaks Italian; and fanaticism speaks Basque. Let us smash these instruments of mischief and error!'[30]

As the armies of the French Revolution swept across Europe, they took their Francophone imperialism with them: 'foreign languages! I believe that in future there will be only one language in Europe, that of the French republicans!' was the view of Mercier.[31] Its rivals were dismissed summarily: 'Italian suited to effeminate delights, German the organ of militarism and feudality, Spanish the cant of the Inquisition, English once glorious and free, now the patter of despotism and the stock exchange'.[32] Not surprisingly, the imposition of the French language – and it should be remembered that no one knew at the time that French control of Europe would be of such short duration – provoked vehement reactions. Probably most influential were the fourteen *Addresses to the German Nation*, delivered by the philosopher Johann Gottlob Fichte at weekly intervals during the winter of 1807–8 in the amphitheatre of the Academy of Sciences at Berlin, then under French occupation. They were given a special frisson by the knowledge that only the previous year, a Nuremberg bookseller, Johannes Palm, had been summarily shot on the direct orders of Napoleon for selling an anti-French pamphlet. Fichte said: 'I know very well what I risk; I know that a bullet may kill me, like Palm; but it is not this that I fear, and for my cause I would gladly die.' The sound of French drums in the street outside, as he began his first lecture, no doubt greatly added to the sense of occasion.[33] Published almost simultaneously in huge print-runs, the *Addresses* caused a sensation and became one of the seminal documents of German nationalism in the nineteenth century.[34]

At the heart of Fichte's project to regenerate the Germans was language, for 'men are formed by language far more than language is by men'.[35] In this, and in much else besides, he was closely following Herder. But Fichte shared none of Herder's cultural pluralism. The German language was unique, he believed, because only the German language had remained pure. All the others had been polluted to a greater or lesser extent by their assimilation into the Latin culture of the Roman Empire: 'the Germans still speak a living language and have done so ever since it first streamed forth from nature, whereas the other Teutonic tribes speak a language that stirs only on the surface yet is dead at the root'.[36] For this reason, the Germans had a special mission to redeem mankind from the abyss into which it had tumbled: 'of all modern peoples it is you in whom the seed of human perfection most decidedly lies and to whom the lead in its development is assigned. If you perish in your essentiality, then all the hopes of the entire human race for salvation from the depths of its misery perish with you'.[37] Although censorship prevented him from naming names, the presence of the French occupation force in Berlin left no one in any doubt as to the identity of his target. When war had broken out in 1806 he had volunteered his services to the Prussian army as a chaplain, promising to preach to the troops with 'swords and lightning bolts'.[38]

Fichte's belief in the linguistic superiority of the Germans was both nationalist and populist. 'In Germany all culture has proceeded from the people (*Volk*)', he declared.[39] Here too he was following Herder's lead in shifting the location of cultural value in any community from the elites to the common people, who formed 'the greatest, more sensual part of mankind'.[40] What the educated classes paraded as evidence of their classical knowledge was nothing more than a meretricious bird of paradise, all show and no substance, fluttering around in the sky and never touching the ground. The culture of the *Volk*, on the other hand, was better likened to an oak, with a rough exterior but deep roots, majestic branches, magnificent foliage and a long life. Folk art, folk dancing and folk songs were not to be despised for their roughness but treasured for their authenticity. They were the 'archives of a nationality', the 'national soul' and 'the living voice of the nationalities, even of humanity itself'.[41] Wilhelm Grimm went even further: 'Only folk poetry is perfect. God himself wrote it as he did the Ten Commandments; it was not pieced together like the mere work of man'.[42]

Herder had been inspired not by direct experience of folk poetry but by the example of the Englishman Thomas Percy, who in 1765 published three volumes entitled *Reliques of Ancient English Poetry, consisting of Old Heroic Ballads, Songs, and other Pieces of our Earlier Poets (chiefly of the Lyric kind), together with some few of the later date*. He had done so apologetically, stating in his preface that the 'extreme simplicity' of the contents suggested that they had been 'merely written for the people'. Only the importunity of his friends had eventually persuaded him to agree to publication, in the hope that the 'artless graces' of the verses would compensate for the want of 'higher beauties'.[43] Herder, on the other hand, was a man with a mission. Popular ballads were not 'the dregs of fairy-tales, superstitions, songs, and crude speech' derided by the sophisticated. On the contrary, without the *Volk* and its culture, there would be 'no public, no nation, no language and no poetry which is ours and lives and works in us'.[44]

This populist view of culture was to prove immensely influential. As Goethe wrote: 'Herder taught us to think of poetry as the common property of all mankind, not as the private possession of a few refined, cultured individuals'.[45] He himself demonstrated what this could mean with, for example, his poem 'Rose upon the Heath' (*Heidenröslein*) of 1771:

> There was a boy saw a little rose grow,
> A little rose on the heath.
> He saw it was so fresh and fair
> And stood still to look at it,
> And stood in sweet joy.
> Little rose, little rose, little rose red,
> Little rose on the heath.
>
> The boy said: I will pluck you,
> Little rose on the heath.
> The little rose said: I will pierce you,
> So you always think of me
> And remember that I will not allow it.
> Little rose, little rose, little rose red,
> Little rose on the heath.
>
> Nevertheless the rough boy plucked
> The little rose on the heath.
> The little rose resisted and pierced him.

Georg Friedrich Kersting, *Caspar David Friedrich in his studio*

With the outside world blocked out and his studio reduced to the bare essentials, Friedrich looks inside himself for inspiration.

Philipp Otto Runge, *Rest on the Flight to Egypt*

Here Runge gives visual expression to Schelling's dictum that 'Nature is visible Spirit; Spirit is invisible Nature'.

Henry Fuseli, *The Nightmare*

For the romantics, the night time was the right time for the subconscious to reveal itself in dreams. Fuseli believed that 'dreams are one of the most unexplored regions of art'.

Karl Friedrich Schinkel, *A Medieval Town on a River*

This depiction of the union of king, church and people presents allegoricall victorious Frederick William III of Prussia returning from the Napoleonic

Anne-Louis Girodet de Roucy-Trioson,
Ossian Receiving the Ghosts of the French Heroes

The poems attributed to the mythic Caledonian bard 'Ossian'
were modern forgeries, but that did not prevent him becoming
a cult for romantics across Europe.

Caspar David Friedrich, *Tombs of Ancient Heroes*

In his characteristically subtle and allusive manner,
Friedrich predicts the doom of the Napoleonic Empire.

J.M.W. Turner,
*The Great Fall of
Reichenbach*

The romantics agreed with
Byron that Switzerland
was 'the most Romantic
region in the world'.

Eugène Delacroix, *Scenes from the Massacres at Chios*

Images such as this of Turkish atrocities inspired Europe-wide support for the Greeks in their struggle for independence.

Francisco de Goya y Lucientes, *The Second of May 1808*

On the Puerta del Sol in Madrid, Spanish insurgents attack
Mamluke soldiers of the French army of occupation . . .

Francisco de Goya y Lucientes, *The Third of May 1808*

. . . and on the following day they face the firing squad.

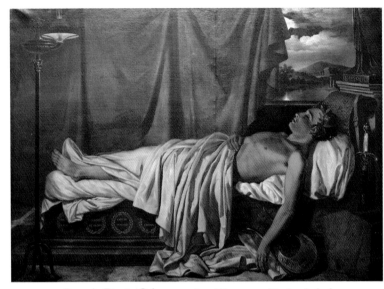

Joseph-Denis Odevaere, *Lord Byron on his death-bed*

The poet as martyred freedom-fighter, hailed by Goethe as 'the greatest genius of the century'.

Francesco Hayez, *The Refugees of Parga*

Betrayed by the British, the Greeks of Parga leave for exile rather than submit to Muslim rule, but their example inspired Italian patriots such as Hayez to resist their own oppressors.

But afterwards in the pleasure
He forgot the pain.
Little rose, little rose, little rose red,
Little rose on the heath.

As his most recent biographer has observed, 'Goethe could hardly have come closer to the impossible, to writing a true folk-song'.[46] Herder published it in 1773, claiming it was from memory, enhancing its 'folk' status by implying it had passed to him via oral transmission. The strophic structure and the repetition of the last two lines ensured that it would be set to music again and again, most famously by the eighteen-year-old Franz Schubert in 1815.

Whether it was collecting folk songs or writing verse in the style of folk songs, populism became an integral part of romantic literature. Surprisingly precocious when it came to collecting was Russia, where as early as 1735 the court poet Vasily Trediakovski had drawn attention to the importance of the 'natural, ages-old poetry of the simple people'[47] and Mikhail Chulkov had published several large collections of fairy tales and folk songs in the 1760s and 1770s.[48] Russian folklore then found its way into the European mainstream through the influence it exerted on poets, especially Alexander Pushkin. In his first major work, *Ruslan and Lyudmila* (1820), Pushkin drew on traditional linguistic sources ranging from Church Slavic to vernacular Russian to create the perfect medium of his fantastic tale of the rescue of the Kievan Princess Lyudmila from the evil dwarf-magician Chernomor.[49]

In Germany, Ludwig Achim von Arnim and Clemens Brentano's collection *The Boy's Magic Horn* [*Des Knaben Wunderhorn*], published between 1805 and 1808, quickly became a 'cult book' for romantics.[50] In a postscript the editors told their readers that the aim of their collection had been to conjure up 'the fresh morning air of old-German times'. They also injected a political note by observing that the rage for novelty in France had led to the virtual extinction of folk songs even before the Revolution – and perhaps had even made that Revolution possible.[51] That Achim von Arnim and Brentano engaged in what might be called 'creative editing', altering metre and spelling and even rewriting, did not detract from its colossal and enduring impact. Over the next century or so, hundreds of musical settings of its 200-odd poems were composed by, among others, Brahms, Britten, Bruch, Eisler, Ives, Gounod, Humperdinck, Mahler, Mendelssohn, Reger, Reichardt, Schoenberg, Schreker, Schumann, (Richard) Strauss, Weber, Webern and Zemlinsky, to mention only the more celebrated.[52]

At least one of these demonstrated that populism could also be popular. This was Carl Maria von Weber (1786–1826), who steeped himself in German folk songs, singing them to his own guitar accompaniment.[53] The most successful result was his romantic opera *Der Freischütz*, first performed at the new Playhouse (Schauspielhaus) at Berlin in 1821. In one number after another, Weber showed how to make art seem artless. Explaining his success, an anonymous contributor to a Berlin musical periodical wrote: 'It was the innermost emotions (*Gemüth*) of the folk that created folk songs and so the folk sees them as its children and loves them with its whole heart'.[54] In reality, none of the melodies with which the work abounds were taken from the *Volk* but such was his command of the idiom that Weber managed to make them seem so. He succeeded so well, indeed, that the premiere was one of the greatest operatic triumphs of the nineteenth century and the work's success was enduring. Thirty different productions had been staged by the end of 1822, while in London by 1824 three different productions were running simultaneously.[55] Its populist appeal was very well captured by Richard Wagner in a review he wrote for a Leipzig newspaper of a performance in Paris in 1841:

Oh, my magnificent German fatherland, how can I help loving you, how can I help adoring you, even if only because it was on your soil that *Der Freischütz* was written! How can I help loving the German people, the people that loves *Der Freischütz*, that even today still believes in the wonder of the most naive fairy-tale, that even today, when it has reached its maturity, continues to experience that sweet, mysterious trembling which made its heart throb when it was young! Oh, how wonderful is German dreaming, and its rapture over visions of forests, of the evening, of the stars, of the moon, of the clock on the village church striking seven! Happy is the man who can understand you, who can believe, feel, dream and share your rapture with you! How happy I am to be German![56]

Wagner went on to tell his readers that when the orchestra played the dance music at the end of Scene One, he had burst into tears as he felt his heart being pierced 'like a thrust from a voluptuous dagger'. As the peasants danced their way into the inn to the strains of a folksy-sounding but in fact cunningly scored 'Walzer', they left the hero – and Wagner – alone with his problems.

In the English-speaking world, the single most influential exercise in populism was probably the preface written by Wordsworth for the *Lyrical Ballads, with a Few Other Poems* he published together with Coleridge in 1798. It was their intention, announced Wordsworth, 'to choose incidents and situations from common life, and to relate or describe them, throughout, as far as was possible in a selection of language really used by men'. Subject-matter from 'humble and rustic life' had been chosen, he went on, 'because, in that condition, the essential passions of the heart find a better soil in which they can attain their maturity, are less under restraint, and speak a plainer and more emphatic language'. As the common people were 'less under the influence of social vanity, they convey their feelings and notions in simple and unelaborated expressions'.[57] However, whether the two most celebrated poems of the collection, Coleridge's 'The Rime of the Ancyent Marinere' and Wordsworth's 'Lines Written a Few Miles above Tintern Abbey' were composed using 'language really used by men' may be doubted.

THE HISTORY OF THE PEOPLE

Much more authentic-sounding was the contemporary poetry of Robert Burns (1759–96), written in language that was unmistakably Scottish but comprehensible to the English. 'Robert Bruce's March to Bannockburn' is a good example, not least because it shows that a people has a history as well as a language:

> Scots, wha hæ wi' Wallace bled,
> Scots, wham Bruce has aften led,
> Welcome tæ yer gory bed,
> Or tæ Victorie!

Now's the day, and now's the hour:
See the front o' battle lour,
See approach proud Edward's power –
Chains and Slaverie!

Wha will be a traitor knave?
Wha will fill a coward's grave?
Wha sæ base as be a slave?
Let him turn and flee!

Wha, for Scotland's king and law,
Freedom's sword will strongly draw,
Freeman stand, or Freeman fa',
Let him on wi' me!

By Oppression's woes and pains!
By your sons in servile chains!
We will drain our dearest veins,
But they shall be free!

Lay the proud usurpers low!
Tyrants fall in every foe!
Liberty's in every blow! –
Let us do or dee!'

Better known by its opening lines – 'Scots, wha hae' – the poem became the unofficial national anthem of Scotland when sung to the traditional tune 'Hey Tuttie Tattie'. In August 1793 Burns wrote to his friend George Thomson that the thought that 'Hey Tuttie Tattie' had been played at Bannockburn 'warmed me to a pitch of enthusiasm on the theme of

Liberty & Independence, which I threw into a kind of Scots Ode, fitted to the Air that one might suppose to be the gallant ROYAL SCOT'S address to his heroic followers on that eventful morning'.[58] Although later displaced by the more melodious 'Scotland the Brave' and more recently still by the rugby song 'Flower of Scotland', it retains quasi-official status by being the favoured anthem of the Scottish National Party. In these six stanzas several of the main themes of romantic nationalism appear: 'the other' in the shape of the invading English ('proud Edward's power'); the nation as suffering martyr ('By Oppression's woes and pains!'); the enemy within ('Wha will be a traitor knave?'); liberation ('Liberty's in every blow!'); nihilism ('Let us do or dee!'); and history ('Scots, wha hæ wi' Wallace bled, / Scots, wham Bruce has aften led'). These historical references are to Sir William Wallace, executed by the English in 1305, and on whose life the film *Braveheart* was loosely – very loosely – based, and Robert the Bruce, who led the Scots to victory at Bannockburn in 1314 and thus secured Scottish independence.

Less radical but even more popular were the historical romances of Walter Scott, whether in the form of verse or novels. Of the twenty-three novels he wrote between 1814 and his death in 1832, only three are not set in the past. As Trollope observed, Scott succeeded in making novel writing respectable by putting history, which was serious, together with the novel, which was not.[59] His ability to combine strong characters in evocative settings with gripping plots made him the most popular writer of the age, not just in Britain but across the world. His narrative poems were 'phenomenal best-sellers' and by 1818 he was making the colossal sum of £10,000 a year from his novels.[60] By the time of his death, the first of the latter –

Waverley – had been translated into French, German, Italian, Hungarian, Swedish, Danish and Russian.[61] In France a sixty-volume edition of his works published in the course of the 1820s sold one and a half million copies in six years.[62]

Among the many literary examples of his fame, the characteristically ironic tribute paid by Stendhal in *The Charterhouse of Parma* stands out: to re-establish his credentials when in exile, the fugitive Fabrizio del Dongo was required to choose a monarchist as a confessor; avoid anyone with a mind of his own; avoid cafés; never read a newspaper; pay court to an attractive noblewoman (to prove that he was not a misanthropic conspirator); and express contempt for all books written after 1720 (with the exception of the novels of Sir Walter Scott).[63] As this implies, Scott was no threat to the established order. A conservative Unionist, he used his stories to promote the reconciliation of Scots and English, Protestants and Catholics, creating in the process 'a synthetic Scot with a Lowland head but in Highland dress'.[64] For that reason most of his novels were set in relatively recent times, with the Jacobite insurgencies to the fore. As Peter Fritzsche has observed: 'The great achievement of Walter Scott was not simply to have produced the effects of historicity in his fictions, but to have drawn attention to the "just passed" quality of a still half-remembered age'.[65]

This use of history was obviously not the invention of the romantics. All these characteristics could be found, for example, in the masque *Alfred* first performed in 1740, with a libretto by James Thomson and David Mallet and music by Thomas Arne, the major difference being that it was English rather than Scottish history that was being celebrated.[66] Nor was the preceding period bereft of 'straight' history. The allegedly unhistorical nature of the Enlightenment is hard to sustain in the light of masterpieces such as Voltaire's *Essai sur les mœurs*, Gibbon's *Decline and Fall of the Roman Empire* and Hume's *History of England*.[67] In his own lifetime Hume won fame and fortune much more from his history than from his philosophy and claimed: 'I believe this is the historical age and this is the historical nation'.[68] Of Gibbon, Sir John Plumb wrote: 'after Gibbon history was fully fledged'.[69]

On the other hand, the romantics, and especially the Germans among them, did approach history in a significantly different way. Gibbon may well have interpreted history 'in purely human terms' (Plumb), but his perspective was that of the enlightened, sceptical, urbane scholar, deploying his superlative literary skills to deride the intolerance and superstition of Christianity and to point the way to a more rational order, as in: 'the various modes of worship, which prevailed in the Roman world, were all considered by the people as equally true; by the philosopher as equally false; and by the magistrate as equally useful. And thus toleration produced not only mutual indulgence, but even religious concord'.[70] Not without reason, the romantics believed that the Enlightenment approached history from the outside, imposing on the past contemporary standards and a contemporary agenda. For their part, they took their cue from the observations about 'characteristic art' by Goethe quoted above.[71] General ideas such as those advanced by Gibbon they dismissed as grand-sounding labels for subjective prejudices. To view a phenomenon from the outside was to invite certain misunderstanding: it had to be illuminated from the inside on its own terms. 'From the inside out' was the only way. Hence Leopold von Ranke's celebrated dictum that 'every age enjoys a direct relationship to God'. No better summary of this essentially romantic position has been produced than Hugh Trevor-Roper's, in the course of an assault on scientific history:

We exist in and for our own time: why should we judge our predecessors as if they were less self-sufficient: as if they existed for us and should be judged by us? Every age has its own social context, its own intellectual climate, and takes it for granted, as we take ours. Because it was taken for granted, it is not explicitly expressed in the documents of the time: it has to be deduced and reconstructed. It also deserves respect ... To discern the intellectual climate of the past is one of the most difficult tasks of the historian, but it is also one of the most necessary. To neglect it – to use terms like 'rational', 'superstitious', 'progressive', 'reactionary', as if only that was rational which obeyed our rules of reason, only that progressive which pointed to us – is worse than wrong: it is vulgar.[72]

The belief that the Enlightenment was hostile to history properly understood could only be intensified by the French Revolution. At first, its aggressive rejection of the past and passionate embrace of universalism, exemplified by the Declaration of the Rights of Man and Citizen, fired the enthusiasm of intellectuals right across Europe. Not for the last time Wordsworth found the most memorable form of words:

> Bliss was it in that dawn to be alive,
> But to be young was very heaven! – Oh! times,
> In which the meagre, stale, forbidding ways
> Of custom, law, and statute, took at once
> The attraction of a country in romance!
> When Reason seemed the most to assert her rights,

> When most intent on making of herself
> A prime Enchantress – to assist the work
> Which then was going forward in her name![73]

But Wordsworth was writing in 1804, by which time events in France had turned his youthful enthusiasm into equally radical rejection. Regicide, civil war, the Terror, dechristianisation, war, imperialist conquest and the looting of Europe combined to turn the liberating enchantress into a destructive demon. The view expressed by the Revolution's chief ideologue, Sieyès, that 'the alleged truths of history have no more validity than the alleged truths of religion',[74] had lost its appeal. It was Edmund Burke's alternative – 'people will not look forward to posterity who never look back to their ancestors'[75] – that had gained in popularity. As Lord Acton observed in his seminal article on 'German Schools of History' in the very first issue of the *English Historical Review* in 1886, at the heart of the Revolution had been 'condemnation of history' and 'the romantic reaction which began with the invasion of 1794 was the revolt of outraged history'.[76] It was also Acton's view that the historicism of romanticism had 'doubled the horizon of Europe' by enlarging its perspective to embrace 'the whole inheritance of man'.[77] The elevated status now accorded to history was well summed up by Thomas Carlyle in his essay of 1830, 'On History': 'History, as it lies at the root of all science, is also the first distinct product of man's spiritual nature; his earliest expression of what can be called Thought'.[78]

As the revolutionaries of 1789 had set off boldly and confidently to establish a new order based on the principles of liberty, equality and fraternity, they threw away the old regime's rule-book: 'let us not be discouraged because we find nothing in history that can be adapted to our present situation', proclaimed Sieyès in *What is the Third Estate?*.[79] For the romantics, who always preferred organisms to artefacts, it was only the past that could provide a guide to present and future. The notion that there was some sort of natural law, eternally and universally valid, was a chimera. Law was not precept but tradition, the organically evolving expression of a community's identity. In Friedrich Schlegel's pithy formulation: 'the world is not system but history'.[80] This historical concept of law was then given magisterial and highly influential expression in Friedrich Carl von Savigny's pamphlet *On the Calling of our Age for Legislation and Jurisprudence* [*Vom Beruf unserer Zeit für Gesetzgebung und Rechtswissenschaft*] published in 1814, in which he argued that law, like all other manifestations of the human spirit, including religion and language, was the fruit of historical development.[81]

MEDIEVALISM

This historicism expressed itself in a re-evaluation of past epochs. The Enlightenment had venerated the classical world just because it was there that the natural laws of aesthetics had been discovered and practised. Many of the romantics admired the Greeks too, but less for their 'noble simplicity and calm grandeur' (Winckelmann) than for their celebration of the wild Dionysian realm and, as we shall see later, the importance they attached to myth. The romantics' attachment to particularism, organic growth and history ensured that they would also find value in other epochs, notably the Middle Ages so derided by the neo-classicists of the Enlightenment. As Kenneth Clark put it: 'To the eighteenth century the middle age was a foggy sea with but one landmark – the Norman Conquest – round which the Gothic cathedrals drifted like rudderless ships'.[82] Winckelmann found that the mere sight of the great Gothic spire of St Stephen's Cathedral in Vienna was like 'a great needle sticking into his eye'.[83] Yet, as we have seen, the equally obtrusive spire at Strassburg gave Goethe just the reverse experience, as it did to the many German romantics for whom the cathedral became an irredentist symbol.[84] Subsequently, enthusiasm for Gothic art and architecture became one of the chief distinguishing marks of the romantics. All those characteristics derided by the classicists – irregularity, ornamentation, gloom, clericalism, transcendentalism – were now paraded as inspiring assets. Especially eloquent was François-René de Chateaubriand, who found his way back to the Catholic Church after his experience of the French Revolution. In *The Spirit of Christianity, or the Beauties of the Christian Religion*, written in exile in London in the 1790s and first published in 1802, he wrote that: 'one cannot enter a Gothic cathedral without feeling a kind of shiver of awe and a vague sentiment of the Divinity'. He went on to explain the appeal of the Gothic by reference to its relationship to history and nature:

The forests of the Gauls have passed in their turn into the temples of our ancestors, and the woods of our oaks have thus maintained their sacred origin. These vaults carved in foliage, these buttresses supporting the walls and terminating abruptly like broken tree trunks, the coolness of the vaults, the shadows of the sanctuary, the dark aisles, the secret passages, the low doorways: everything in the

Gothic church retraces the labyrinths of the forest and excites feelings of religious horror, the mysteries and the Divinity.[85]

The book proved to be highly influential. As David Cairns has written: 'it set a current of sympathy flowing between the author and a whole generation of young French men and women, kindling their imagination over a wide range of feelings and ideas ... More than any other work, it was the primer of early French romanticism'.[86]

From being a term of abuse, as in 'O more than Gothic ignorance!' (the epithet applied to the boorish Squire Western by his sophisticated sister in Henry Fielding's novel *Tom Jones* of 1749), 'Gothic' became a badge of pride, as in the title of Horace Walpole's novel – *The Castle of Otranto, A Gothic Story* of 1764. The latter was one of the first signs that the cultural tide was on the turn. Inspired by a nightmare (a very romantic origin in itself), it included such extravagances as a portrait that stepped down out of its frame, a statue that bled, a sword so massive that it needed fifty men to wield it, giant severed body parts, a sundry cast of magicians, goblins, friars and other agents of the supernatural, and so on. Both the original dream and the writing of the novel took place in the ideal environment, for in the course of the previous fifteen years or so, Walpole had turned his house at Strawberry Hill near Twickenham into a Gothic extravaganza. Dismissed by one architectural historian as 'a witty sham, an immense curiosity cabinet of architectural fragments heaped up into a building',[87] Strawberry Hill nevertheless initiated a trend that was to last for a century and more.[88]

In his study of the 'Gothic Revival', first published in 1950, Kenneth Clark maintained that it was 'an English movement,

perhaps the one purely English movement in the plastic arts'.[89]
There is only one reference to Goethe in the book, in a
footnote to a passage in which he writes about Gilbert Scott's
study of the German Gothic in the 1840s and comments:
'Germany was not yet awake to the Gothic Revival'.[90] This
majestic ignorance can perhaps be attributed to the ignorance
of youth (he had just completed his studies at the University
of Oxford). In reality, the Germans were in the van and,
moreover, went far beyond the castellated walls and pointed
arches that decorated the English Gothic villas and sham
castles. Twenty years before Scott began his researches, Hegel
was giving lectures at the University of Berlin on, among many
other things, 'what is called Gothic or German architecture',
in the course of which he gave credit to Goethe for having
rescued it from the reputation for crudity and barbarism.[91] He
also succinctly summed up its appeal to the romantics: 'while
the buildings of classical architecture in the main lie on the
ground horizontally, the opposite romantic character of Christian churches consist in their growing out of the ground and
rising to the sky'.[92]

The last part of that observation could well serve as an
epigraph for *A Medieval City on a River*, painted by Hegel's
near-contemporary and fellow-Berliner Karl Friedrich
Schinkel in 1815. The cathedral rises naturally, as if growing
out of the oak forest that surrounds it. To emphasise its organic
character, its second spire is still under construction, like all
romantic art a work in the process of becoming, not a completed artefact. In the foreground a prince rides home from
the wars to his castle, situated symbolically immediately
opposite the cathedral, as his loyal subjects rush to greet him.
As the storm clouds disperse above an idealised medieval city,

a rainbow forms to herald better times to come.[93] As the date of its creation reveals, this was an allegory on the return of King Frederick William III from the Napoleonic Wars and the liberation from French domination he had helped to achieve.

The image of an unfinished cathedral had a special resonance for Germans, for the greatest of all their medieval buildings, Cologne Cathedral, was just that. Not least because of its gigantic size, work had faltered in the mid-fourteenth century and had come to a complete stop by the middle of the sixteenth, with just the choir (itself big enough to be a cathedral), side aisles and two storeys of the south tower completed. The survival of a medieval crane on the latter was a visual reproach to succeeding generations. Yet it was just this disjunction between medieval aspiration and modern achievement that made such a powerful impression on the romantics. One of the earliest and most eloquent to respond was the naturalist Georg Forster, who among many other things had accompanied Captain Cook on his second expedition to the South Pacific. A free-thinker of Protestant origins, it was an aesthetic not a religious experience that he sought when he entered Cologne Cathedral: 'whenever I am in Cologne I always visit this wonderful temple, in order to experience the shivering excitement of the sublime'.[94] The clusters of slender columns in the choir appeared to him 'like the trees of a primeval forest' and the vaults 'like crowns of branches'. Anticipating Hegel by a generation (he was writing in 1790), he commented that in Greek architecture was to be found the essence of all that was human and the here-and-now; the pillars of Cologne soaring through the Gothic gloom were manifestations of another world, 'fairy palaces' bearing witness to the creative power of mankind.[95]

Forster concluded by expressing his profound regret that such a magnificent building should have been left unfinished. He died in Paris four years later, bitterly disappointed with the French Revolution he had supported so enthusiastically at long range. So he did not live to see a campaign for the completion of Cologne Cathedral become the great *cause commune* of the German romantics. To the fore was another disillusioned 'German Jacobin', Joseph Görres, who had turned from radical politics to Catholicism and nationalism. He made the first public appeal in his periodical *Rheinischer Merkur* in November 1814, or in other words during the triumphalist period of self-congratulation following the defeat of Napoleon at the Battle of Leipzig the previous year which led to the liberation of Germany from French rule.[96] Not one of the innumerable projects for victory monuments should be realised, he argued, until the standing reproach that was the uncompleted cathedral had been corrected. He received powerful support from the leading lights of German romanticism, notably Friedrich Schlegel (who had written his own paean of praise to the cathedral in his treatise on the 'Principles of Gothic Architecture' in 1805)[97] and the brothers Sulpiz and Melchior Boisserée, who had done so much to further the cause of medieval painting.[98] Despite his well-known dislike for what he thought were the excesses of the romantics, even Goethe was induced to put his shoulder to the wheel.

Eventually it moved, not least because the Boisserée brothers had converted the Crown Prince of Prussia to their cause.[99] Alas, he did not succeed to the throne until 1840, but then set about making amends. In a grand ceremony on 4 September 1842, King Frederick William IV dedicated the cornerstone of the resumed construction. He also took the

*Cologne Cathedral as it was when construction resumed in
1842 and how it was to look when completed.*

opportunity to make one of the public speeches he was so good at, hailing the project as a symbol of German power and unity: 'The spirit which builds these portals is the same which broke our fetters twenty-nine years ago, which brought to an end the humiliation of the Fatherland and the alien occupation of this province. It is the spirit of German unity and strength ... I pray to God that the Cathedral of Cologne may soar over this city, may soar over Germany, over ages rich in peace until the end of time'.[100] Even with the help of the state, another thirty-eight years were to pass before the completed cathedral could be dedicated in 1880 by Frederick William's brother, the new German Emperor William I.

LANDSCAPE AND MYTH

By the time the cornerstone of the cathedral was laid in 1842, the river above which it towers had itself become the object of a cult. For the Enlightenment, the Rhine was the 'Pfaffengasse' or 'clerics' alley', the notoriously backward region dominated by the prelatical princes of Cologne, Trier, Mainz, Worms and Speyer. Visitors to Cologne derided the superstitious locals, especially their fabulous collection of relics, which included the remains of the three Magi, of a thousand martyrs slaughtered during the reign of the Emperor Maximianus and, even more improbably, of 11,000 virgins who came from Britain to convert the locals only to be martyred by the Huns in AD 383.[101] The sceptical rake William Beckford wrote in 1783 that the pious burghers of Cologne 'care not a hair of an ass' ear whether their houses be gloomy, and ill contrived; their pavement overgrown with weeds, and their shops with filthiness;

provided the carcases of Caspar, Melchior and Balthazar [the three Magi] might be preserved with proper decorum'.[102] But once Beckford started travelling up the Rhine, his contempt turned into admiration: 'let those who delight in picturesque country, repair to the borders of the Rhine, and follow the road which we took from Bonn to Coblentz. In some places it is suspended, like a cornice, above the waters, in others, it winds behind lofty steeps and broken acclivities, shaded by woods, and cloathed with an endless variety of plants and flowers'.[103] Beckford has been claimed as 'the first Rhine romantic', for it was from that point that the river became a favourite destination for British tourists.[104]

And they wrote about it, enthusiastically. Of such accounts, two stand out for being among the biggest best-sellers of the period. The first was Byron's *Childe Harold's Pilgrimage*, the poem that brought him fame and fortune overnight. As he put it in a letter to his friend Tom Moore in March 1812, he 'awoke one morning and found himself famous'. Moore's own version was: 'his fame had not to wait for any of the ordinary gradations, but seemed to spring up, like the palace of a fairy tale, in a night'.[105] Byron travelled up the Rhine in the spring of 1816 and was bowled over by 'the perfection of mixed beauty' he found there. The stretch from Bonn to Mainz he found 'beautiful – & much surpassing my expectation ... nothing can exceed the prospects at every point'.[106] In the third canto of *Childe Harold*, published later that year, he gave these impressions poetic form:

> ... true Wisdom's world will be
> Within its own creation, or in thine,
> Maternal Nature! for who teems like thee,

Thus on the banks of thy majestic Rhine?
There Harold gazes on a work divine,
A blending of all beauties; streams and dells,
Fruit, foliage, crag, wood, cornfield, mountain, vine,
And chiefless castles breathing stern farewells
From gray but leafy walls, where Ruin greenly dwells.[107]

In 1818 a very different kind of best-seller propagated the same message. This was Mary Shelley's *Frankenstein*, the passage on the Rhine being based on a journey she had made with Percy Shelley four years earlier. Although the Shelleys had had to put up with the company of some 'disgusting Germans', who 'swaggered, and talked, and, what was hideous to English eyes, kissed one another', she extolled what she saw as 'the loveliest paradise on earth'.[108] In her novel, the same sort of words were put into the mouths of Victor Frankenstein and his Swiss companion Henry Clerval, who exclaimed that the beauties of the Rhine exceeded even those of his native country – 'He felt as if he had been transported to Fairy-land, and enjoyed a happiness seldom tasted by man'.[109]

As enthusiasm for things German began to gain momentum during the middle decades of the nineteenth century, so did the rush of British tourists anxious to experience 'the most romantic spot on earth'.[110] Ironically, the desire to experience untamed nature and ruined castles was satisfied by such instruments of modernity as the railways and steamships, which made the journey increasingly quick, comfortable and cheap. Soon the Rhine was being used as a metaphor for the special qualities of German culture, as in Edward Bulwer Lytton's novel *The Pilgrims of the Rhine*, for example, in which one of the characters observes as the boat travels upriver from

Cologne: 'As the Rhine flows, so flows the national genius, by mountain and valley – the wildest solitude – the sudden spires of ancient cities – the mouldered castle – the stately monastery – the humble cot. Grandeur and homeliness, history and superstition, truth and fable, succeeding one another so as to blend into a whole'.[111]

French attitudes towards the Rhine were more ambivalent, not least because the whole of the left bank had been part of France from the conquests of 1794 to the collapse of the Napoleonic empire twenty years later. Handing back so much of the Rhineland at the final peace settlement in 1815 stuck in the craw of many French patriots. However, although they came to it rather late, the French romantics eventually succumbed to the Rhine's attractions. In 1842 no less a figure than Victor Hugo published a travelogue devoted solely to the region: 'above all rivers, I love the Rhine ... this proud and noble river, impetuous without fury, wild, but majestic ... a noble river, at once feudal, republican, and imperial'.[112] In a passage that was purple even by Hugo standards, he went on: 'The Rhine combines every quality a river can exhibit. The rapidity of the Rhone, the breadth of the Loire, the rocks of the Meuse, the sinuosity of the Seine, the translucency of the Somme, the historical reminiscences of the Tiber, the regal dignity of the Danube, the mysterious influence of the Nile, the golden sands of the glittering streams of the New World, the phantoms and legends of some Asiatic stream'.[113]

The Rhine was only one of many locations to excite the enthusiasm of the romantics. Competing for pre-eminence as the quintessentially romantic landscape was the river's source – the Alps. Viewed in the past as an inconvenient obstacle to travellers, to be traversed as quickly as possible, in the late eighteenth century it was just their rugged inaccessibility that began to give them such appeal. To the fore, as usual, was Rousseau, who increasingly shunned cities for the countryside, the wilder the better: 'It is already clear what I mean by fine country. Never does a plain, however beautiful it may be, seem so in my eyes. I need torrents, rocks, firs, dark woods, mountains, steep roads to climb or descend, abysses beside me to make me afraid. I had these pleasures and I relished them to the full, as I came near to Chambéry'.[114] What he liked best about the high Alps was that they presented Nature in a form least polluted by man. It was there that the hero of his epistolary novel *La Nouvelle Héloïse*, Saint-Preux, had his mystical experience and wrote to his doomed lover Julie: 'It seems that in being lifted above human society, one leaves below all base and terrestrial sentiments, and that as [a man] approaches the ethereal regions, his soul acquires something of their eternal purity'.[115]

As the biggest best-seller of the eighteenth century,[116] *La Nouvelle Héloïse* did more to publicise the appeal of the Alps than any other publication. It also encouraged Alpine tourism. In the course of the eighteenth century, the pace of international travel increased rapidly. If still frequent, wars were more localised and less destructive. If still defective, roads were better. If still risky, travel was no longer so perilous. So the 'Grand Tour' came to be regarded as an essential part of a gentleman's education. The first English traveller to leave an account of a journey to the continent that was a tour rather than a pilgrimage was Sir Thomas Hoby, who visited Italy in 1549.[117] But it was in the eighteenth century that the trickle of English visitors became a flood and then a torrent. In 1768 Baretti estimated that during the previous seventeen years, some 10,000 English people had travelled to Italy.[118] By 1770 one anonymous observer could write: 'where one Englishman travelled in the reign of the first two Georges, ten now go on a Grand Tour', while Edward Gibbon estimated fifteen years later that there were 40,000 English travelling on the continent (although this must have been a guess and was almost certainly an over-estimate).[119]

Most of them went to Italy via the Alps. 'Foreigners arrive in droves', wrote the Swiss artist Caspar Wolf in 1779 in the preface to his collection of engravings entitled *Detailed Description of the Remarkable Views of Switzerland*.[120] It was intended to show those who could not travel there in person what they were missing. It was a service also performed by many of the travellers themselves, including such distinguished painters as John Robert Cozens and Francis Towne, who in the same year – 1781 – painted Alpine scenery.[121] It was the sight of Cozens' watercolours that inspired Turner to travel to the Alps in 1802 when the Peace of Amiens opened up the continent again, albeit briefly, to English travellers. As he told the painter Joseph Farrington, whom he met in the Louvre on his way home, he had found the Alps 'very romantic'.[122]

The Alps were everything the romantics liked – irregular, particular, sublime, organic, terrifying, spiritual. The Swiss natural scientist Horace-Bénédict de Saussure, only the third person to reach the summit of Mont Blanc, in 1786, wrote of his experiences in the high mountains: 'the soul ascends, the vision of the spirit tends to expand, and in the midst of this majestic silence one seems to hear the voice of nature and to become certain of its most secret operations'.[123] It was an emotion repeated by the English romantic poets who found Switzerland 'the most Romantic region in the world', as Byron put it. Together with his new friend Shelley, whom he had just met at Sechéron near Geneva in 1816, he went on a boating trip equipped not with a guidebook but with a copy of *La Nouvelle Héloïse*.[124]

Coleridge exclaimed when seeing the Alps at Chamonix: 'who would be, who could be an atheist in this valley of wonders?' Shelley could, but even he was overwhelmed by the same sights: 'I never imagined what mountains were before ... the immensity of these aerial summits excited, when they suddenly burst upon the sight, a sentiment of ecstatic wonder not unallied to madness'. The poetic result was his *Ode to Mont Blanc*, a mountain he had climbed in the company of none other than Saussure:

> Dizzy Ravine! and when I gaze on thee
> I seem as in a trance sublime and strange
> To muse on my own separate fantasy.

In the preface to Mary Shelley's *History of a Six Weeks' Tour* (1817), he wrote: 'the poem was composed under the immediate impression of the deep and powerful feelings excited by the objects which it attempts to describe; and, as an undisciplined overflowing of the soul, rests its claim to approbation on an attempt to imitate the untameable wildness and inaccessible solemnity from which those feelings sprang'.[125]

At about the same time some romantics were going south to the Alps, others were going north to the Scottish Highlands, also in pursuit of wild, rugged, untamed landscape. It was not until the definitive pacification in the wake of the failed Jacobite rebellion of 1745 that the region became safe enough to be visited without a military escort. In the 1760s its appeal was greatly enhanced by the sensational success of three volumes of 'prose translations' of verse purporting to have been composed in the third century AD by 'Ossian', the son of Fingal, the great Caledonian hero whose band of warriors had defeated an invading army. They were published by a school-teacher, James Macpherson, whose modest role in the enterprise was affirmed in the title of the first volume: *Fragments of Ancient Poetry, Collected in the Highlands of Scotland and Translated from the Galic or Erse Language*. The preface gave an unequivocal assurance that 'the public may depend on the following fragments as genuine remains of ancient Scottish poetry'. Although the exact date could not be established, 'tradition, in the country where they were written, refers them to an æra of the most remote antiquity; and this tradition is supported by the spirit and strain of the poems themselves'. The verses, it was claimed, had been handed down from one generation of bards to another.[126] The first 'fragment' begins:

Vinvela: My love is the son of the hill. He pursues the flying deer. His gray dogs are panting around him; his bow string sounds in the wind. Whether by the fount of the rock, or by the stream of the mountain thou liest; when the rushes are nodding with the wind, and the mist is flying over thee, let me approach my love unperceived, and see him from the rock. Lovely I saw thee first by the aged oak of Branno, although thou wert returning tall from the chace; the fairest amongst thy friends.[127]

Although one modern scholar has dismissed Ossian's work as 'totally unreadable ... of inexpressible tedium; its characters as bloodless as the ghosts who provide its supernatural machinery',[128] many contemporaries hailed him as a Scottish Homer.

Moreover, it was not only in Scotland itself that he received an ecstatic reception. An early boost was supplied by no less a writer than Goethe in *The Sufferings of Young Werther*. At what proves to be their very last meeting, Werther reads to Lotte some of Ossian's songs in his own translation, at her request. They have an electrifying effect: 'A flood of tears, which burst from Lotte's eyes and gave her oppressed heart relief, checked Werther's reading. He threw down the papers, seized her hand, and wept the bitterest tears. Lotte rested her head on the other hand and hid her eyes with her handkerchief. Both were in a fearful agitation'.[129] When he resumed reading, it was not long before she completely lost control: 'Her senses grew confused, she pressed his hands, pressed them against her breast, bent down with a sorrowful movement to him, and their glowing cheeks touched. The world was lost to them'. Not for long, alas, and Lotte was soon hurrying from the room, telling Werther she could not see him again. He shot himself the next day.

By the end of the century, Ossian's poems had been translated into Italian, French, German, Polish, Russian, Danish, Spanish, Dutch, Czech and Hungarian, or in other words into more languages than any other work written in the English language in the eighteenth century except *Robinson Crusoe*.[130] As Matthew Arnold later wrote, it poured 'like a flood of lava through Europe'.[131] In 1770 Herder wrote to a friend: 'should I ever reach the coasts of Britain, I shall only hurry through, see some theatre and Garrick, and say hello to Hume, and then it will be up to Wales and Scotland, and on to the Western Isles, on one of which sits Macpherson, Ossian's youngest son'.[132] Yet from the very start, loud and influential voices had been raised casting doubt on the authenticity of the poems.

The derision heaped on them by Dr Johnson might be dismissed as yet another example of his notorious dislike for all things Scottish. Possibly also tainted was the vigorous criticism voiced by Irish scholars enraged that their own heroes had been reassigned to Scotland. It was a different matter when David Hume disowned his earlier endorsement and told his fellow-Scot James Boswell that the poems were all fakes, adding that he would not believe that *Fingal* was an ancient poem 'though fifty bare-arsed Highlanders' should swear to it.[133]

Indeed it was not an ancient poem. Macpherson had not 'collected' *Fingal* or *Temora* (the other epic poem in the collection) but had written them himself, or – more likely – had translated them from Gaelic poems written by his cousin Lachlan Macpherson, the laird of Strathmashie, with the assistance of Ewart Macpherson.[134] This question continues to exercise literary scholars[135] but need not delay us here. What was significant about the Ossian phenomenon was the widespread and enduring response it evoked right across Europe, although it might be added that this alone suggests that the poems attributed to him had both more literary merit and more historical substance than sceptics such as Hugh Trevor-Roper are prepared to concede. At least three major paintings testify to their evocative power: Gérard's *Ossian Evoking Phantoms by the Sound of his Harp* (1801), Girodet's *Ossian Receiving the Ghosts of the French Heroes* (1802), and Ingres' *The Dream of Ossian* (1813). All three were commissioned by Napoleon, who took Ossian's poems on both his first overseas expedition (to Egypt) and his last (to St Helena).[136] Napoleon was also a great admirer of Jean-François Le Sueur's opera *Ossian, or The Bards*, first performed shortly after the new Emperor's coronation in

1804. Its colossal success – it was given seventy performances during the next decade – confirmed Le Sueur's position as the leading composer of the Napoleonic regime.[137]

The poems had been available in French translation since 1777,[138] which greatly helped Ossian's fame to spread across the continent. The need to discover, revive or, if necessary, invent ancient folk epics proved to be ubiquitous. *The Tale of Igor's Campaign*, an epic poem written in Old East Slavic, discovered in 1791 in a monastery and published in 1800, gave Russian nationalists the cultural pedigree they felt they needed. Dating from the 1180s, it recounts a campaign led by Prince Igor of Novgorod against Turkic nomads. Despite doubts raised periodically, it is almost certainly authentic.[139] It was given a warm reception by contemporaries, as was Kirsha Danilov's *Ancient Russian Verse* published four years later.[140]

Just as influential but much less trustworthy were the various discoveries announced a little later in the Bohemian Lands of the Habsburg Empire, where cultural competition between Germans and Czechs intensified rapidly during the first quarter of the nineteenth century. When Count František Kolovrat, the Governor of Bohemia, founded the National Museum in 1818, his manifesto, written in German, referred to the new institution as a 'Patriotic Museum' (*vaterländisches Museum*), but when Josef Jungmann translated this into Czech, it became the 'National Czech Museum' (*Národní české museum*).[141] In the previous year, the folklorist Václav Hanka announced that he had discovered an ancient Slavonic manuscript in a vault under the church at Dvůr Králové. Although it was lying under a sheaf of arrows that had been there since the days of the great Hussite warrior Jan Žižka, it was thought to be much older.[142] A fragment of a much larger work, the poems it comprised told the Czechs what they knew already but never tired of hearing again and again: that they had a very ancient culture and that their past had been distinguished by feats of heroic resistance to German-speaking intruders. In a poem called simply 'Patriotism', for example, the great warriors Zaboj (Destroyer) and Slavoj (Glorious) unite to defeat the wicked German oppressor Ludiek, whom Zaboj kills in single combat.[143]

This collection became known as the 'Královédorský Manuscript'. Of even greater importance was 'The Judgment of Libuše' (later known as the 'Zelenohorský Manuscript'), sent anonymously the following year, 1818, to Count Kolovrat.[144] That they were both forgeries concocted by Hanka did not prevent them winning general acceptance. Indeed they spawned a number of lesser forgeries, composed specifically to lend them greater authority.[145] Hanka, who successfully sued a newspaper unwise enough to question their authenticity, achieved the status of a national hero. When he died, his funeral was attended by 20,000 people, 400 torch-bearers and prominent Czechs from every walk of life.[146] As his fellow-forger brazenly asserted, the creators of 'pious lies' did 'far more to contribute to our culture than men who depopulate centuries of our history with excessive criticism'.[147]

In the meantime, Hanka's forgeries had proved to be 'a pivotal event in the history of Czech nationalism'.[148] Among those who followed his coffin was the most important Czech leader of the first half of the nineteenth century, František Palacký, who had noted in his diary in 1819: 'with inexpressible joy I read the KM [Královédorský Manuscript] for the first time early this summer ... How you have been transformed in your glory, O Motherland! Once more you have held high your noble head, and nations look to you with admiration'. Age did not dim this emotion. Forty years later he wrote: 'We, the older contemporaries who had witnessed and participated in the effort to forge and cultivate a literary Czech language prior to 1817, can tell you how the discovery of the KM opened a new world before us at a stroke, an unsuspected world'.[149]

The manuscripts provided material for painters and musicians as well as poets and novelists. When the National Theatre in Prague was opened on 11 June 1882, the work chosen to celebrate the occasion was Smetana's *Libuše* with a libretto by Josef Wenzig, who had been heavily influenced by the forged manuscripts. It was less an opera than a musical pageant celebrating the Czech foundation myth of the ninth century, when the eponymous heroine finds a husband in the sturdy peasant Přemysl, thus founding the great Czech dynasty that was to rule the Bohemian Lands for the next four centuries. In the final scene, Libuše recounts a series of visions in which the glorious, if troubled, future of the Czechs is revealed. When she reaches the era of the Hussite persecutions, mists begin to rise and her eyes grow dim, but she concludes: 'this much I feel and know in the depths of my heart: my dear Czech people will never perish, they will be able to resist all the horrors of hell!' – 'including the beastly Germans and their Austrian Habsburg masters', the audience may well have added to themselves as they rose to their feet to cheer.[150]

The Germans had their own myths, of course, and it was no coincidence that it was during the romantic era that they flourished. Of the rich abundance available (the Grimm brothers collected more than five hundred), three were especially popular. The first concerned the great medieval Emperor Frederick Barbarossa (1122–90). He had not really drowned while on the Third Crusade, it was maintained. He had been transported miraculously to a cave under the Kyffhäuser Mountain in Thuringia, where he sat sleeping, waiting until the German nation called on him in its hour of need.[151] Although Germany was eventually united without the visible assistance of Barbarossa, a grateful Veterans' Association raised a colossal monument eighty metres high to him on the Mountain.

More dynamic was the myth of Hermann (Arminius in Latin) the Cheruscan, the leader of the Germanic tribes which had inflicted a shattering defeat on the Roman legions led by Varus in the Teutoburg Forest in AD 9. It was a myth that had enjoyed an initial burst of fame during the early sixteenth century, not coincidentally another period of nationalist excitement. In 1529 the Lutheran patriot and humanist Ulrich von Hutten wrote a dialogue entitled *Arminius* in which the hero argues his case in the court of the dead, winning a place of honour as 'Brutus Germanicus', a freedom-fighter against foreign domination.[152] Interest then waned during the confessional and civil strife that afflicted the Holy Roman Empire for most of the following century and more and did not revive until the middle of the eighteenth century. Inspired by Ossian, Friedrich Gottlieb Klopstock composed a major trilogy: *Hermann's Battle* (1769), *Hermann and the Princes* (1784) and *Hermann's Death* (1787). Among the German virtues to which Klopstock gave poetic form were modesty, chastity, piety, humanity, morality and devotion to justice, duty and self-sacrifice.[153] This combination of martial glory and ethical self-congratulation proved irresistible, making Klopstock's version of the myth an immediate and durable influence. Extracts found their way into almost all anthologies of the late eighteenth century and were still being used to inspire enthusiasm for the patriotic cause in the War of Liberation of 1813.[154]

Klopstock and the other Hermann-authors also constructed a set of semiotic references to characterise German national identity. Against the urban order and sophistication of the Romans, they opposed the rough, untamed wilderness of the German forests. In Klopstock's *Hermann's Battle*, nature itself joined in on the German side, sending torrential rain and a thunderstorm to impede the Romans' advance, before hemming them in with river and forest, as carrion-crows swept down from the sky, shrieking for blood, and the eagles sang the song of revenge.[155] The most popular of these natural images was the oak-tree, symbol of German strength, antiquity and durability:

> O Fatherland! O Fatherland!
> You are like the greatest,
> All-encompassing oak,
> In the deepest grove of the forest,
> The tallest, oldest, most sacred oak,
> O Fatherland![156]

This topographical association was frequently employed. Writing to his future wife in 1772 during a visit to the Teutoburg Forest, Herder linked geography, history and national character:

I am now in the country, in the most beautiful, the most rugged, the most German, the most romantic region of the world. The very same field on which Hermann fought and Varus was defeated; still an awful, rugged, romantic valley surrounded by singular mountains. However much of the German valour and of the Klopstockian ideal of morality and greatness may be lost, the soul is nevertheless disposed by the daring singular demeanour of this Germany to believe that there is a beautiful, rugged German nature.[157]

Experience of the French Revolution and Napoleon, especially the humiliating defeat inflicted on the Prussians at Jena and Auerstedt in 1806, led to a radicalisation of the Hermann myth. The most extreme statement was made by Heinrich von Kleist in his play *Hermann's Battle* in 1808. He took all the elements from earlier versions – liberty, hatred, revanchism, bloodthirstiness, the contrast between Germanic virtue and Roman vice – and intensified them to a pitch that can only be called pathological. As the Roman legions approach through Cheruscan territory, reports are brought in of looting, burning and horrendous atrocities. For example, a Roman soldier who became involved in a dispute with a woman who had just given birth, tore the baby from the mother's breast and used it to club her to death; when told, his commander simply shrugged his shoulders. Another eye-witness reported that the Romans had felled a thousand-year-old sacred oak, dedicated to Wotan. The Cheruscans who tried to resist had their villages burned down. Far from being appalled, Hermann is delighted and adds to the horror stories, insisting that it be spread around, that the Romans also made the Cheruscans get down on their knees to worship Roman Gods. Indeed, he then gives orders that Cheruscans disguised as Romans should go out and burn and plunder where the Romans had not been.

As this suggests, Kleist's Hermann will stop at nothing to achieve the total defeat and annihilation of the enemy. On hearing that a Cheruscan maiden has been gang-raped by a group of Roman soldiers and has then been killed by her own father, he commands the latter:

> Take your violated virgin daughter to your hut!
> There are fifteen German tribes
> So take your sharp sword and
> Cut her body into fifteen pieces.
> Send with fifteen envoys a piece
> To each of Germany's fifteen tribes.
> I shall give you fifteen horses.
> For your revenge this will recruit
> Throughout Germany and
> The storm-winds that blow through the forests
> Will cry out: insurrection!
> And the waves that beat the shore
> Will roar: Liberty!
>
> *The Cheruscan People*
> Insurrection! Revenge! Liberty![158]

At the other end of the scale in terms of stridency lay Caspar David Friedrich's painting of 1812, *Tombs of Ancient Heroes*. It depicts a remote, overgrown ravine in which a number of tombs appear to have been placed at random. The inscriptions on the sarcophagi convey a patriotic message – 'Peace be on your grave, Saviour in time of need'; 'Noble youth, Saviour of the Fatherland'; and 'Noble Sacrifice for Liberty and Justice'. Coiled around the broken gravestone in the foreground, which is marked 'ARMINIUS', is a snake in the colours of the French tricolour. Whether Hermann's tomb has been vandalised or whether he himself has broken out, the message is clear: the French chasseurs, to be seen in the background at the entrance to the cave, are doomed.[159] When Friedrich painted the picture in 1812 he could not have known that Napoleon was about to suffer the catastrophe in Russia that led to the collapse of his Empire. Yet even after he had been defeated by the allied powers at Leipzig in October 1813, Friedrich did not change his allusive style. In *The Chasseur in the Woods* of 1814 he simply depicts the French chasseur standing lost in the middle of a forest, dwarfed by the pine trees that symbolise death, as a raven on a tree stump croaks out his doom.[160]

The third great German myth and, as it turned out, artistically the most productive, was *The Song of the Nibelung*. Written down by an anonymous poet in the Danube region between Passau and Vienna in the late twelfth century, it drew on a much older oral tradition. Indeed, the very lack of an identifiable author commended itself to the romantics, for, as Jakob Grimm put it in his essay on the work, this absence 'is usual with all national poems and must be the case, because they belong to the whole people'.[161] Rediscovered in an Austrian library in 1755 and translated from Middle High German into modern German almost at once, it took a generation or so to win acceptance. At least there was no dispute as to its authenticity, as thirty-five different manuscripts surfaced eventually, eleven of them essentially complete. With his habitual contempt for his native literature, Frederick the Great dismissed it 'as not worth a shot of gunpowder' but by the 1790s it was being hailed as the German *Iliad*.[162] It went through countless editions, in both verse and prose forms, and was even published in a pocket-edition so that soldiers could

Peter Cornelius, Hagen Sinks the Hoard of the Nibelungen
in the Rhine *(1859)*

take it with them on campaign.[163] It soon became the most
illustrated of all literary works, with the sole exception of
the Bible, attracting, among others, Heinrich Fuseli, Peter
Cornelius, Carl Philipp Fohr and Julius Schnorr von
Carolsfeld.[164]

Of all the creative artists to be inspired by *The Song of the
Nibelung*, the most ambitious was, of course, Richard Wagner.
His four-part music-drama *The Ring of Nibelung*, written and
composed between 1848 and 1874 and performed in its entirety
for the first time at Bayreuth in 1876, stands as one of the
towering achievements of European culture. One does not

have to agree with W.H. Auden that Wagner was 'one of the greatest musical geniuses who ever lived'[165] to appreciate its power. Wagner's *The Ring* is emphatically not a musical setting of *The Song*. As he told Princess Marie Wittgenstein with engaging candour in 1857: 'What happens with me is that I seldom actually read what's in front of me, but rather what I want to read into it'.[166] In fact, he took even more from the Icelandic sagas, most notably the *Edda*, in both verse and prose forms, and the *Volsung Saga*. But what emerged was unmistakably all Wagner.

It was not so much the plot or the characters of the sagas that caught his attention as their mythic status. Myth, he came to believe, 'is true for all time, and its content, however compressed, is inexhaustible throughout the ages'.[167] Myth alone, because of its symbolic nature, was able to deal with past, present and future and remain eternally and universally valid: 'what is incomparable in myth is the fact that it is always true and, in its most concentrated compression, is inexhaustible for all ages. It is the task of the poet just to interpret it'.[168] In myth, 'the conventional form of human relations, only explicable by abstract reasoning, disappears almost completely. Instead, only that which is eternally comprehensible and purely human appears in an inimitable concrete form'.[169] In effect, in *The Ring* Wagner was seeking to fulfil the hope of Novalis (from whom he took a great deal) that one day there would come a time: 'when the world will be returned to a life free unto itself ... and man will recognise in myth and poem the true eternal world history'.[170]

CONSERVATIVES AND REVOLUTIONARIES

Many if not most romantics liked myth because it was profound, particularist, populist and simultaneously national and universal. As usual, Wordsworth found the perfect poetic expression when writing about the Prometheus myth in *The Excursion*:

> Fictions in form, but in their substance truths,
> Tremendous truths! familiar to the men
> Of long-past times, nor obsolete in ours.[171]

This affinity with history and myth was often conducive to a conservative attitude towards the affairs of the day. The romantic reaction against the rationalism of the Enlightenment could only be intensified by the excesses of the French revolutionaries. Georg Forster, the admirer of Cologne Cathedral, was also an enthusiastic supporter of the French Revolution – in principle. It was with the slogan *'ubi bene ibi patria'* that he rallied to the new regime when the French conquered Mainz in October 1792. The rigours inseparable from military occupation began his disillusionment, a visit to Paris completed it. Shortly before his death there in January 1794, he wrote: 'the world is facing the tyranny of reason, of all kinds perhaps the most remorseless ... The nobler and more excellent the cause, the more devilish is its abuse. Fire and flood, every kind of damage inflicted by fire and water, are nothing compared with the havoc that reason will wreak'.[172]

Of all the visual depictions of the gulf that opened up between the rhetoric of the French Revolution and its practice, none were more eloquent than those produced by Goya. As we have seen, his attitude towards the Enlightenment was not at all clear. First-hand experience of occupation by the armies of Napoleon gave him both the subject-matter and the passion to create two of the most violent images of war ever created – *The Second of May* and *The Third of May* – to celebrate the rising against the French and its brutal repression. Goya himself wrote that his intention was: 'to perpetuate with my brush the most notable and heroic actions or events of our glorious revolution against the tyrant of Europe'.[173] In the first, a group of insurgents are shown attacking French soldiers on the Puerta del Sol in Madrid. In the foreground one insurgent stabs a Mamluke as he pulls him from his horse, as another thrusts his sword into the horse's shoulder. In the second and better known painting, on the following day a French firing-squad executes a group of insurgents. To the left sprawls a heap of bodies already despatched, to the right another group waits its turn. The religious element is accentuated by the outstretched arms of the central victim, the friar kneeling by his side and the great monastery that dominates the dark skyline. There is no stoic heroism here, only anguish, despair, anger and the fear of death. The contrast with Jacques-Louis David's contemporary glorification of Napoleon and his wars could not be more stark.[174] Even more brutally unequivocal were the etchings collectively known as *The Disasters of War*, in which Goya shows terrible scenes of mutilation, murder and rape.

For those denied the opportunity to witness the effects of the Revolution at first hand, it was possible to maintain support for its principles. Secure in his comfortable bachelor existence at the University of Königsberg on the easternmost edge of the German-speaking world, Kant never ceased to maintain that revolutionary France had acted on behalf of all mankind in seeking to emerge from self-incurred immaturity – but equally never ceased to be a loyal subject of his employer, the King of Prussia. Hegel was closer to the action, but he too had no difficulty in separating his philosophy from his politics. In 1822 at the same time that he was asking the Prussian authorities to take action against a periodical in which his philosophy had been criticised, he was praising the French Revolution for marking the moment when man realised he could reshape reality in accordance with thought. Every 14 July without fail he drank a glass of red wine to celebrate the anniversary of the fall of the Bastille.[175]

Neither philosopher, of course, can be assigned to romanticism, despite Kant's emphasis on self-determination and Hegel's remarkable ability to articulate its goals. Most German romantics rejected the Revolution and all its works. Among the most flamboyant were the 'Nazarenes', a group of painters who formed a self-consciously backward-looking 'Brotherhood of St Luke' in Vienna in 1809. In the following year they moved to Rome, but not to the Rome of classical civilisation but the Rome that was the world capital of Christianity. Indeed they moved into an abandoned monastery, San Isidoro, and lived a communal life. The conversion of their leader, Johann Friedrich Overbeck, to Catholicism in 1813 dramatised their rejection of the modern world.[176] His paintings and drawings included *The Raising of Lazarus*, *Christ and his Disciples at Emmaus*, *The Entry of Christ to Jerusalem*, *Self-Portrait with Bible*, *Christ with Mary and Martha*, *Dürer and Raphael Clasp Hands before the Throne of the Church*, *The Triumph of Religion in the Arts*, and so on.[177] The contrast with the major painters of neo-classicism could hardly be greater. Representative of

Franz Pforr, Count Habsburg and the Priest *(1809–10)*

the Nazarene approach to art and life was Franz Pforr's *Count Habsburg and the Priest*, symbolising the unity of throne and altar, as the ruler offers his horse to the priest seeking to cross the swollen river to bring the last sacrament to a dying parishioner.[178]

The art of the Nazarenes became immensely popular. Helped by the recent invention of lithography, their images were disseminated right across Germany and Austria. Overbeck was told by a proud parent in 1818 that 'Your name races through every German speaking territory. Political newspapers and other journals bear it from south to north and from west to east. Your Frankfurt Cartoons, and those of the excellent Cornelius, become described in greater and greater detail, and are judged great patriotic achievements'.[179]

The Nazarenes started out as a secession (from the Vienna Academy), indeed arguably represented the first secession movement in European painting, but they ended up well and truly integrated into the establishment. Their studios in Rome were visited by the Crown Prince of Bavaria, Ludwig, in 1818 and by the Austrian Emperor Francis I the following year.[180] The former visit inspired possibly the most informal of all depictions of a prince patronising artists in the shape of Franz Ludwig Catel's *Crown Prince Ludwig in the Spanish Wine Taverna at Rome*.[181] By that time they had already painted a fresco (a medium they favoured just because of its antique nature) for the Prussian consul at Rome. A broad stream of commissions from German princes followed. The most successful of them, Peter von Cornelius, became director of the Academy at Munich, where among many other projects he painted the enormous frescoes commissioned by King Ludwig I for the Ludwigskirche in the Ludwigstrasse.[182]

Also deeply integrated in the political establishment was Adam Heinrich Müller, who started out in the service of Prussia but spent most of his career working as a publicist for the Austrian Chancellor Prince Metternich, by whom he was rewarded with a noble title (Ritter von Nittersdorf). As the chief political theorist among the German romantics, he did more than anyone to encourage an alliance between intelligentsia and state. In a public lecture delivered in 1808 he proclaimed that 'Man cannot be thought of outside the state ... the state is the embodiment of all the needs of the heart, the spirit and the body ... Man can neither hear, see, think, feel nor love without the state; in brief, he is not conceivable other than in the state'.[183] In a series of influential articles published in the *Berliner Abendblätter*, which he edited and mostly wrote with Heinrich von Kleist, Müller argued that academics must abandon their hypercritical and negative attitude, together with their 'sterile, insatiable lust for knowledge'. When the Christian faith stood in all its glory, he went on, then all scholarship had a religious point of reference to give it meaning, but in the present secular age scholarship could only attain the necessary vitality and shape through voluntary service of the state.[184] It need hardly be added that this olive branch was seized with alacrity by the German princes. When Frederick William IV laid the foundation-stone of the south portal of Cologne Cathedral, he was also proclaiming the union of throne, altar and intelligentsia.[185]

Across the Rhine, the French romantics were not inclined to view with favour a revolutionary state which had done so much to demystify the world and which had adopted neo-classicism as its official style. The meretricious vulgarity of the parvenu Napoleon was, if anything, even less to their taste. The angry young French romantics were angry young royalists and clericalists. Alphonse de Lamartine, Alfred Vigny and Victor Hugo were all originally keen supporters of aristocracy, monarchy and Catholicism.[186] Chateaubriand resigned from the service of Napoleon and went into exile when the Bourbon duc d'Enghien was judicially murdered in 1804.[187] During Napoleon's 'Hundred Days', Eugène Delacroix even served as a '*camelot du roi*' or life-guard for Louis XVIII.[188]

The alliance between throne and altar did not last long in France. It could not survive the strain imposed by the returning Bourbons who, as Talleyrand famously remarked, 'had learnt nothing and forgotten nothing'. By the middle of the 1820s, the romantics who had opposed Napoleon and welcomed back Louis XVIII, were beginning to turn. In Honoré de Balzac's novel *Lost Illusions*, set in 1821–2, Lucien Chardon, a young poet from Angoulême, is told on his arrival in Paris that he must take sides in a fierce literary-cum-political battle in which 'the royalists are romantics, the liberals are classicists' and is advised to throw his lot in with the former, because 'the romantics are all young folk and the classicists are periwigs: the romantics will win'.[189] In 1824 Victor Hugo was still speaking of literature as 'the expression of a religious and monarchical society'[190] but it was in that year that the battle-lines shifted decisively, not least because on 16 September Louis XVIII died and was succeeded by his less intelligent but more reactionary brother as Charles X. As if to demonstrate that the cultural climate was turning colder, the director of the Académie française denounced romantic literature in a public session. To add insult to insult, the Rector of the University of Paris, who also happened to be a bishop, then argued at a prize-giving ceremony that once a national literature had attained perfection, as it had done in France during the golden age of Louis XIV, writers should be required to adhere to its precepts.[191]

Hugo found his way to the left through the decompression chamber of admiration for Napoleon, in whose service his father had risen to the rank of general. His *Ode à la Colonne de la Place Vendôme* of 1827 marked a rupture with the Bourbons. Three years later, in the preface to his play *Hernani*, he completed his conversion by writing: 'romanticism, taken as a whole, is only liberalism in literature. Literary liberalism will be no less democratic than political liberalism. Freedom in art and liberty in society are the twin goals to which all consistent and logical thinkers should march in step'.[192] In a letter to Lamartine in the same year he added, referring to romanticism: 'ours too is a question of freedom, it too is a revolution; it will stand intact to walk side by side with its political sister. Like wolves, revolutions don't eat one another'.[193]

In July 1830 that promise was put to the test in the revolution that put an end to the Bourbon monarchy and installed Louis Philippe duc d'Orléans as king. It was a test that the romantics passed, at least in a visual sense, for the street fighting in Paris inspired the most famous of all revolutionary images – Delacroix's *Liberty Leading the People*. This was also the perfect illustration of the famous definition offered by the French art critic Auguste Jal in his book on the Salon of 1827, 'Romanticism in painting is political; it is the echo of the cannon shot of 1789'.[194] Delacroix had already dramatised the revolutionary nature of his romantic vision by exhibiting *Scenes from the Massacres at Chios* at the Salon of 1824. This depicted the atrocities committed by Turks on the island of Chios in 1822, which had become a *cause célèbre* of the Greek War of Independence. At the left, a group of prisoners awaits transportation to slavery; at the right, a child tries to suckle the breast of its dead mother; dominating all is a Turkish rider who has tied a young girl to his horse and is drawing his scimitar to strike down her imploring mother. The painting's impact was enhanced by being exhibited alongside Ingres' *Vow of Louis XIII*, which presented as great a contrast as it is possible to imagine. Three years later, the two artists again offered the chance to compare classicism with romanticism when they exhibited *The Death of Sardanapalus* and *The Apotheosis of Homer* respectively.

Also in 1827 Delacroix had painted another powerful image drawn from the Greek war – Greece expiring on the ruins of Missolonghi, although it was not exhibited at the Salon. It was not only a statement of support for the Greek struggle for independence, but was probably also a lament for Byron, who had died at Missolonghi in 1824.[195] It was not an isolated tribute. Byron's contribution to giving European romanticism a radical flavour was colossal. His visits to the Eastern Mediterranean in 1809 and 1810 turned him into an enthusiastic campaigner for Greek independence from Turkish rule. There was nothing new about that, but his ability to express his philhellenism in powerfully poetic language gave it immense and lasting force. *Childe Harold's Pilgrimage* advertised the cause with the following lines that instantly became famous:

> Fair Greece! sad relic of departed worth!
> Immortal, though no more; though fallen, great!
> Who now shall lead thy scatter'd children forth,
> And long accustom'd bondage uncreate?[196]

Even more famous were the lines from *Don Juan*, published nine years later:

> The mountains look on Marathon –
> And Marathon looks on the sea;
> And musing there an hour alone,
> I dream'd that Greece might still be free;
> For standing on the Persian's grave,
> I could not deem myself a slave.[197]

By that time, Byron had left England in disgrace and high

dudgeon, hounded out by persistent rumours of sexual misconduct, including incest with his half-sister. His exile did nothing to diminish his impact, at home and abroad. As much thrilled as repelled by the air of danger and scandal that accompanied him on his journeys, Europeans turned him into a cult figure. In his *Méditations Poétiques*, published in 1820 and often regarded as the start of French romanticism, Alphonse de Lamartine expressed his disapproval of Byron's cynicism but in a way that amounted to admiration: 'you, whom the world is still unable to name, mysterious spirit, mortal, angel or demon, whoever you are, Byron, good or bad spirit, I love the savage harmony of your music, as I love the way the thunderbolt and winds mix during the storm, together with the noise of the torrents!'[198] Intellectuals as diverse as Goethe and Heine, Pushkin and Mickiewicz, paid tribute to his demonic genius. The most authoritative came from Goethe – 'Byron is the greatest genius of the century ... He is not antique, he is not modern; he is like the present day'.[199]

It was ironic that Byron was regarded as the romantic hero *par excellence*, for, as Maurice Bowra has written, he was not really a romantic at all, rather a survivor from the eighteenth century having more in common with Pope (or even Dryden) than with Keats or Wordsworth.[200] If, as Bowra maintains, it was the importance assigned to the imagination that distinguished the romantics, then Byron disqualified himself, for he wrote with a characteristic jeer: 'It is the fashion of the day to lay great stress upon what they call "imagination" and "invention", the two commonest of qualities: an Irish peasant with a little whisky in his head will imagine and invent more than would furnish forth a modern poem'.[201] As Keats wrote to his brother in 1822: 'You speak of Lord Byron and me –

There is this great difference between us. He describes what he sees – I describe what I imagine. Mine is the hardest task. You see the immense difference'.[202] Ironic, sarcastic, sceptical and cynical, Byron would have been a short-priced favourite in any competition to find the poet who least resembled Novalis.

But Byron did believe passionately in the Greek cause and it was he who turned philhellenism into a European movement.[203] So, when the Greek War of Independence began in 1821, European public opinion was ready to give it enthusiastic support. Byron's death at Missolonghi on 19 April 1824, albeit from fever rather than enemy action, sealed his heroic status. His images had circulated widely during his lifetime, but after his death their popularity was rivalled only by those of Napoleon.[204] If his influence on the movement that led eventually to Greek independence in 1832 cannot be assessed with any precision, it was certainly great. The historian of the philhellene movement has written: 'to the philhellenes in action, he was a practical inspiration; to the Greeks he was a poet, a hero, and a god. His contribution to the liberation of Greece is literally incomparable'.[205]

As the old regimes restored after the fall of Napoleon turned increasingly reactionary, so were the romantics driven leftwards. Even in relatively liberal Great Britain (or the United Kingdom, as it should be known following the Union with Ireland in 1801), the repression of social and political radicalism provoked a strong reaction from the younger romantics. A particular bugbear was Lord Castlereagh, of whom Shelley wrote in *The Masque of Anarchy*:

> I met Murder on the way –
> He had a face like Castlereagh –

Very smooth he looked, yet grim;
Seven bloodhounds followed him.
All were fat; and well they might
Be in admirable plight,
For one by one, and two by two,
He tossed them human hearts to chew
Which from his wide cloak he drew.[206]

When Castlereagh died by his own hand in 1822, Byron wrote of his grave in Westminster Abbey:

Posterity will ne'er survey
A nobler grave than this:
Here lie the bones of Castlereagh:
Stop, traveller, and piss.[207]

This engagement with the political world was common to many of the British romantics. Wordsworth told a visitor that 'although he was known to the world as a poet, he had given twelve hours thought to the conditions and prospects of society, for one to poetry', while Shelley wrote to a friend: 'I consider Poetry very subordinate to moral & political science, & if I were well, certainly I should aspire to the latter'.[208] While Wordsworth, Southey and Coleridge were propelled from left to right by the impact of the French Revolutionary and Napoleonic Wars, the younger generation never stopped attacking the establishment. In his *Ode to Liberty* of 1820 Shelley wrote:

Oh, that the free would stamp the impious name
Of King into the dust! or write it there,

So that this blot upon the page of fame
Were as a serpent's path, which the light air
Erases, and the flat sands close behind![209]

At least George IV was a native. Elsewhere in Europe, alienation from the regime was especially acute where it was associated with foreign occupation. Already in 1815 the Austrian military commander in Italy, Count Heinrich von Bellegarde, warned Metternich that 'the men of spirit and letters are trying to write with a common purpose, which under an academic form hides the political aim of making Italy its own master, an idea which is disturbing even as a Utopia'. The image of Austrian rule, personified by Metternich, was as unromantic as could be imagined, so – as the poet Silvio Pellico remarked – to be a romantic was to be a liberal, for 'only ultras [conservatives] and spies dare call themselves classicists'.[210] It was an association the Austrians themselves confirmed when they closed down the leading romantic periodical *Il Conciliatore: foglio scientifico-letterario* in 1819.[211]

Geographical proximity to the Greeks' struggle for liberation from Turkish rule naturally gave encouragement to Italians wishing to follow their example. Particularly stimulating was a well-reported episode in 1818 when the inhabitants of Parga were forced to leave their homes after the British had handed over the town to the Turks. This inspired at least two major works, the first being Giovanni Berchet's epic poem *The Refugees of Parga*, written in exile in London in 1821 and published in 1824. Berchet had already composed the first manifesto of Italian romanticism in 1816, in the shape of his *Semi-Serious Letter from Grisostomo to his Son*.[212] The second was one of the most memorable of all Italian romantic paint-

ings, Francesco Hayez's *The Refugees of Parga*. It was commissioned by Count Paolo Tosio of Brescia, who originally
asked for something classical. Hayez persuaded him to allow
a modern subject, commenting later that 'among the many
[subjects] that crowded into my mind, I gave preference to the
topic of the refugees from Parga, a subject that represented
patriotic feelings that were very well suited to our condition'.[213]

As this suggests, Hayez and his fellow-patriots had no
difficulty in identifying themselves with the oppressed Greeks
and their Austrian masters with the Turkish oppressors. This
simple transfer mechanism proved to be a useful way of evading
censorship, favoured especially by Italy's favourite art-form –
opera. Nowhere else in Europe and at no other time in European history has so much opera been performed as in Italy
between 1815 and 1860. In Milan there were six theatres in
which opera was performed regularly, in Naples there were
five plus one more occasional venue.[214] Looking back from
1869, one contemporary observed: 'no one who did not live in
Italy before 1848 can imagine what the opera house meant in
those days. It was the only outlet for public life, and everyone
took part. The success of a new opera was a capital event that
stirred to its depths the town lucky enough to have witnessed
it, and word of it ran all over Italy'.[215] When Italian opera
audiences saw the Gauls resisting the Romans (in Bellini's
Norma) or the Children of Israel resisting the Babylonians (in
Verdi's *Nabucco*) they knew that it was their own heroic struggle
for liberty that was really being depicted on stage.[216] As we
have seen, the Czechs in Bohemia were engaged in a very
similar enterprise when they too opposed what they perceived
to be Austrian oppression.[217]

In German-speaking Europe, the gulf between state and

society was less wide. The policies dictated by Metternich and imposed by the German princes with varying degrees of enthusiasm certainly aroused resentment but at least the oppression was home-grown. Moreover, it was first and foremost political. In many German states it was accompanied by cultural policies and patronage that could only win the approval of the intelligentsia. Whether it was Frederick William III of Prussia buying Caspar David Friedrich's paintings for the Crown Prince or Ludwig I commissioning major works of art from the Nazarenes or Frederick Augustus I of Saxony appointing Richard Wagner as his director of music, there were enough positives to promote at least an ambivalent attitude towards the regimes. This was summed up best by the liberal politician Friedrich Dahlmann who likened the Prussian state to 'the magic spear that heals as well as wounds'.[218] Many of the leading German romantics nestled comfortably in the warm embrace of state patronage, for example Schinkel, Schlegel, Müller and Cornelius. Of course there were others who went into internal exile, such as Caspar David Friedrich, or even took to the barricades when insurrections erupted in 1830 and 1848–9. Among this activist group, Wagner stood out for his characteristic extremism, conspiring to incite a violent revolution, buying hand grenades, inciting the Saxon troops to mutiny, and playing an active part in the uprising.[219] He was very lucky to escape to exile in Switzerland with the assistance of his ever-generous friend Liszt.

The experiences of the abortive revolution in Dresden in May 1849 did however turn Wagner away from any thought of cooperation with the existing regime. In *Lohengrin*, completed in 1848, he had portrayed a benevolent but unexciting old regime headed by King Henry the Fowler (*alias* his employer King Frederick Augustus I of Saxony) galvanised by the arrival of the charismatic hero Lohengrin (*alias* Richard Wagner). In the first draft of *The Ring of the Nibelung*, also written in 1848, the chief god, Wotan, is allowed to survive, albeit suitably chastened and educated by the death of his grandson Siegfried and the suicide of his daughter Brünnhilde. After 1849, however, Wotan perishes along with all the other gods in a total bonfire of the old regime.

Wagner's *Ring* presents the most radical and thoroughgoing critique of the modern world attempted by a romantic. It addresses all forms of abusive power, not just the naked despotism to which Alberich aspires but also the less obviously toxic contractual authority exercised by Wotan. In both cases a rape of nature was involved – the former steals the Rhinegold, the latter wrenches a branch from the world-ash tree and fashions it into a spear inscribed with the treaties with which he rules the world. The first crime plunges the Rhine into darkness, the second begins the slow death of the natural world, as the leaves fell, the tree rotted and the well ran dry.[220] In both cases, power can only be bought at the cost of love. It is not only Alberich who renounces love. As Wotan explains to Brünnhilde in a crucial passage in Act Two of *The Valkyrie*:

> When youthful love's
> delights had faded,
> I longed in my heart for power:
> impelled by rage
> of impulsive desires,
> I won for myself the world.[221]

It is love that thwarts Wotan's plans to use a controlled revolution in the shape of his son Siegmund to get the ring back from Alberich. The adulterous and incestuous coupling of Siegmund and his long-lost sister Sieglinde allows Wotan's formidable wife Fricka to intervene in the name of law to ensure that Siegmund is killed by Sieglinde's cuckolded husband Hunding. It is some measure of Wagner's radicalism that he should have portrayed incestuous sex, if not actually on stage then clearly about to occur: the stage direction at the end of Act One of *The Valkyrie* states: 'he pulls her to him with furious passion, she sinks on his chest with a cry', adding 'the curtain falls quickly' ('And about time too!' scribbled an outraged Arthur Schopenhauer in the margin of the copy Wagner had sent him[222]). Perhaps even more arresting was Wagner's indulgent attitude to homosexuality. When his second wife Cosima was rash enough to criticise the relationship between their friend Paul von Joukowsky and his Neapolitan man-servant Pepino, she incurred the Master's disapproval: 'It is something for which I have understanding, but no inclination', Wagner said. 'In any case, with all relationships what matters most is what we ourselves put into them'.[223]

In the course of Wagner's life (1813–83), the world changed more rapidly and radically than at any time in the previous history of the human race. The application of means–ends rationality had transformed the material world. Like most other romantics, Wagner believed that the scientific investigation and understanding of nature had led not to liberation but to conquest and exploitation. Referring to the French, he told Cosima in 1873: 'If only we could reach the point of no longer looking to them for our ideas! ... How low they have sunk one can see by the fact that they imagine they can get things done by maxims based on reason. As if anything ever comes of reason! ... Only religion and art can educate a nation – what use is science, which analyses everything and explains nothing?'.[224] In this, as in so much else in Wagner – as in *all* the other romantics, indeed – the voice of Rousseau can be heard telling us that the advancing reign of reason was only throwing 'garlands of flowers over the chains which weigh us down'.[225] Were they able to return to the twenty-first century to witness the effects of the further advances of scientific rationalism, their worst fears would be confirmed.

CONCLUSION: DEATH AND
TRANSFIGURATION

Death and Transfiguration is a tone-poem composed by Richard Strauss in 1888. Sixty years later, in 1948, the year before he died at the age of eighty-five, he quoted the 'transfiguration' theme in 'At Sunset', one of his 'Four last songs'. Strauss's long career illustrated as well as anything the longevity of romanticism in music. He was also a living as well as a sonic link with an earlier generation, for he attended the first performance of *Parsifal* at Bayreuth in 1882 at the age of eighteen.[1] He – and all the other composers writing in a romantic idiom deep into the twentieth if not the twenty-first century – confirm E.T.A. Hoffmann's dictum that 'music is the most romantic of all the arts, one might almost say the only one that is genuinely romantic'.[2]

In the non-musical genres, on the other hand, the romantic revolution had faded away by the middle of the nineteenth century, by which time the Prussian novelist Theodor Fontane could announce: 'romanticism is finished on this earth; the age of the railway has dawned'.[3] In 1848, 'the year of revolutions', the radical poet Ferdinand Freiligrath took farewell of romanticism:

> Your reign is over! Yes, I do not deny it,
> A spirit different from yours now rules the world,
> We all can sense how it blazes a new trail,
> It throbs through life, it blazes before our eyes,

It strives and struggles – so let no one stand in its
   way![4]

The Enlightenment, it seemed, had had the last laugh after all. Modernisation could not be arrested. The spread of literacy, the improvement of physical communications, the accelerating pace of scientific innovation, the rapid increase in population, urbanisation, the expansion of the public sphere – just to list a selection of the forces at work – combined to promote a sense of sustained secular progress. Moreover, technological change seemed to herald emancipation from more than reliance on the quadruped or Shanks's pony. As Friedrich Harkort, a German industrialist, put it in 1847: 'The locomotive is the hearse that will carry absolutism and feudalism to the graveyard'.[5]

Optimism about the onward march of modernisation was accompanied by pessimism about the short- and medium-term effects. The dislocation caused by industrialisation and urbanisation convinced many observers that the poor were becoming more wretched, more numerous, and more dangerous. This did not mean that all artists became socialists, but it did mean that a growing number of them chose the material conditions of the here and now as their central concern. It was no accident that the literary genre best suited to the new direction, first known as 'realism' and later as 'naturalism', was the novel, for the world of the modern city was prosaic rather than poetic. In works such as Dickens' *Oliver Twist* (1837–9), Gustav Freytag's *Profit and Loss* (1855), Dostoevsky's *Crime and Punishment* (1866), or the twenty volumes of Emile Zola's 'Rougon-Macquart' cycle (1870–93), the wonderful variety of commercialised urban society was

French railway in the mid-nineteenth century. As a middle-class family relaxes, on the other side of the tracks the three props of the old regime, marginalised by the coming of the railway, await their doom: the noble and his chateau, the priest and his church, the peasant and his donkey.

usually less apparent than its attendant squalor and tension. This was the realm of anomie, that sense of moral rootlessness which the French sociologist Emile Durkheim identified as the essence of the human condition in the industrialised world.

Also naturally suited for capturing contemporary reality was painting, which found an articulate spokesman for the new approach in Gustave Courbet, as well as a wonderfully gifted practitioner. Among his trenchant observations on the nature of his art were: 'painting is an essentially *concrete* art and can only consist of the presentation of *real and existing things*', and the quintessentially anti-romantic jibe: 'show me an angel and I'll paint it!'.[6] Although never a propagandist, Courbet was very much a man of the left, a republican and supporter of the revolutionary Commune of 1871, who paid for his beliefs by spending two years in prison and the rest of his life in exile. Together with Jean François Millet, he represented, as it were, the 'heroic' phase of realism, all funerals, firing-squads, hunched peasant women, and horny-handed sons of toil.

This realist trend was underpinned by a positivist belief in the natural sciences. As Zola wrote of the Salon of 1866: 'the wind blows in the direction of science. Despite ourselves, we are pushed towards the exact study of facts and things'.[7] As technological advance was piled on technological advance, especially in the field of communications, and as the publication of *On the Origin of Species* by Charles Darwin in 1859 seemed to deliver the *coup de grâce* to revealed religion, the disenchantment of the world seemed complete. Moreover, it was accompanied by the allied triumph of liberalism. This was the period when Italy and Germany were unified and when liberals took control in one state after another, even in the multinational Habsburg Empire where the great *Ringstrasse* project in Vienna exemplified a new alliance between dynasty, liberal bourgeoisie and material progress.[8]

But no sooner had this new triumph of the culture of reason and progress been proclaimed than the dialectic began its corrosive – and creative – work. In his novel *The Stomach of Paris*, published in 1873, Zola put the following words into the mouth of Claude Lankier, who points first at the iron and glass structure of the recently erected central market – *Les Halles* – and then at the neighbouring medieval church of Saint Eustache, predicting: 'This one will kill that one, for iron will kill stone'. He was not the first materialist to be deluded by the shadows on the wall of the cave: *Les Halles* were demolished in the 1970s, but Saint Eustache still stands.

In the very same year that Zola's Lankier made his hubristic prophecy, a long economic recession began, usually if mis-leadingly called 'the great depression'. Together with the eruption of new mass political forces, with socialism, clericalism and anti-Semitism in the van, it ensured that the high-noon of bourgeois liberalism was of short duration.

It was now that it turned out that romanticism had been resting not dying, as the maxims of an earlier generation were rediscovered. In 1888 the twenty-year-old French painter Émile Bernard virtually repeated the words of Caspar David Friedrich quoted above when he wrote that the artist should not paint what he sees in front of him but the idea of the thing he sees in his imagination.[9] Similarly, the central tenet of what became known as 'symbolism', as expressed by its main organ *Symbolist* – 'Objectivity is nothing but vain appearance, that I may vary or transform as I wish' – could have been said by any romantic two or three generations earlier. The old romantic obsessions with death, the night, and sex were all back in favour again, nowhere more powerfully than in Gustav Klimt's notorious ceiling paintings for the University of Vienna. What the academics had wanted and expected was a portrayal of the victory of reason, knowledge and enlightenment. What they got was a world turned upside down, in which philosophy is subconscious instinct, justice in 'Jurisprudence' is a cowed and helpless victim of the Law and in 'Medicine' behind Hygeia, the Greek goddess of health, lurk more interesting phenomena than personal hygiene and physical fitness, notably sex and death.[10]

This phantasmagoria has much in common with the night-marish visions of Goya, but this is not a simple case of repe-tition. European culture has not repeated itself cyclically but has developed dialectically. High-Victorian positivism was not a re-run of the Enlightenment, nor was *fin de siècle* a repetition of romanticism. No romantic would have adopted the radical 'perspectivism' of, for example, Nietzsche, who did not just privilege subjectivism but denied the very possibility of objectivity: 'So what is truth? A mobile army of metaphors, metonyms, anthropomorphisms – in short an aggregate of human relationships which, poetically and rhetorically heightened, became transposed and elaborated, and which, after protracted popular usage, poses as fixed, canonical, obligatory. Truths are illusions whose illusoriness is overlooked'.[11]

Around the turn of the twentieth century, a reaction to the neo-romantic excesses of *fin de siècle* set in and there emerged a general trend towards aesthetic purification. In music, it can be heard in Arnold Schoenberg's move from the lush post-Wagnerian orchestration of *Gurrelieder* (begun in 1900) to the atonal austerity of *Five Orchestral Pieces* (1909). In architecture it can be seen in the contrast between Antonio Gaudi's *Casa Milá* (1906–10) and Walter Gropius's Bauhaus (1925–6). In sculpture it can be seen in the contrast between the neo-baroque swirls of Auguste Rodin's *Balzac* (1897–8) and the spare simplicity of Constantin Brancusi's *Sleeping Muse* (1910). In painting it can be seen in the contrast between the voluptuous eroticism of Lovis Corinth's *Salome* (1899) and the chaste linearity of Piet Mondrian's *Composition with Gray and Light-Brown* (1918). T.S. Eliot spoke for all modernist artists, and not just for writers, when he claimed: 'the progress of the artists is a continual self-sacrifice, a continual extinction of personality. Poetry is not the turning loose of emotions but an escape from emotion, not the expression of personality but the escape from personality'.[12] It is difficult to imagine a more

Romanticism redivivus: Gustav Klimt, Medicine *(1907).*
Fresco for the University of Vienna, destroyed by fire in 1945.

anti-romantic utterance, or one that was so comprehensively contradicted by everything that Eliot created, which is as original as it is expressive.

The allied victory of 1945 was acclaimed in both West and East as a cultural as well as a military triumph. The discovery of the full horrors of National Socialism engendered a belief in the absolute values of liberalism or communism every bit as self-confident as that entertained by the French Revolutionaries of 1789 or the liberals of the mid-nineteenth century. As Martin Jay has written, 'aesthetic modernism at mid-century, precisely because of its detachment from concrete social and political practice, came to be taken by many as the appropriate cultural expression of a much larger project of human emancipation'.[13] The collapse of the wartime alliance and prolonged struggle between the two victors in an intense ideological cold war helped to maintain the triumphalist impetus, as each side noisily proclaimed its own special virtues and the opposition's defects. Of the visual evidence which confirmed the victory of modernism, perhaps the most obtrusive was the rash of skyscrapers, all in the spare, linear, rational 'international style', which mushroomed across the globe. It was also the clearest indication that modernism at last had found a style in which it felt at home. In the nineteenth century, almost every conceivable style had been tried – neo-Gothic, neo-classical, neo-Renaissance, neo-Egyptian, neo-baroque, neo-everything. Heinrich Hübsch actually published a pamphlet in 1828 asking pathetically *In What Style Should We Build?*.[14] By the middle of the twentieth century, modernism knew what it wanted. One of its most eloquent spokesmen, Nikolaus Pevsner, regarded this development as 'full of promise', posing the rhetorical question: 'Can we not take it then that the recovery of a true style in the visual arts, one in which once again building rules, and painting and sculpture serve, and one which is obviously representative of character, indicates the return of unity in society too?"[15] A comparison between Charles Garnier's wonderfully eclectic Paris Opéra and the bleak Deutsche Oper (German Opera) in West Berlin, designed by Fritz Bornemann and opened in 1961, makes the point well.

The Deutsche Oper opened on 24 September 1961, just six weeks after the erection of the Berlin Wall had begun. The latter was supposed to make the Eastern bloc safe for socialism. With the advantage of hindsight, we can see that the system was doomed. Many were the corrosive forces which brought the wall tumbling down just twenty-eight years later, among them economic failure, the arms race, and the Soviet defeat in Afghanistan, but perhaps the most powerful was advancing communications technology. The evil empires of Hitler, Mussolini and Stalin had benefited from a perfect match between their despotic objectives and the instruments of control available. Without electronic amplification, the radio or the cinema, they could not have cowed so many for so long. By the 1960s, television was eclipsing all other forms of mass media and was proving increasingly difficult to control. The Berlin Wall could keep a people in prison but it could not keep out the images and sounds of western liberty and western consumerism. The two seemed to go together. So when the Soviet Empire collapsed after 1989, media moguls were quick to claim the credit. Looking back from 1997, Ted Turner, then still in charge of CNN, boasted: 'We have played a positive role. Since the creation of CNN, the Cold War has ended, the conflicts in Central America have come to a halt, and peace has come to South Africa.'[16]

But, like other revolutions in communications, television proved to be a double-edged sword. It exposed the inability of the Soviets to control Afghanistan, but it also exposed the inability of the Americans to control Vietnam. It advertised the attractions of consumerism, but also laid bare its excesses. If it inspired the serfs of socialist command-economies to rattle their chains, it also inspired the children of its beneficiaries to bite the hands that fed them. For the post-1945 generation which grew to maturity in the 1960s, modernism had become complacent, middle-aged and – fatal adjective – boring. The eruption of youth culture thrust reason to one side. If it acquired a brief political tinge in 1968 and if its exponents have always been prone to striking moralising postures of a vaguely leftist kind, at the heart of youth culture is anarchic hedonism. Significantly, its preferred medium has been music. Also revealing is the strong emphasis on narcotics, to facilitate escape from mundane reality and its illusory values to the 'wonder world of the night'. So massive is the purchasing power of young people (those aged fourteen to twenty-five account for over 70 per cent of record sales, for example),[17] that what was still a marginal group as recently as the 1950s is now the driving force in consumerist culture.

There has also been a corresponding reaction to the culture of reason at a more intellectual level in the shape of strands known collectively as 'post-modernism'. Thankfully, there is no space to investigate this richly various – and contradictory – phenomenon. It must suffice to assert that all post-modernists have in common a rejection of grand narrative, teleology and rationalism. They squarely belong with the culture of feeling, in a line which stretches back to *fin de siècle* and romanticism (and indeed to the baroque). But, as before, this is not just another spin of the cycle's wheel, but a dialectical progression. Where it will take us next is anyone's guess. That the central axiom of romanticism – 'absolute inwardness' – will have a role to play is certain. The romantic revolution is not over yet.

NOTES

Introduction

1 Joachim Whaley, 'The German lands before 1815', in Mary Fulbrook (ed.), *German History since 1800* (London, 1997), p. 15.

2 'Des tendances de l'art musical à l'époque actuelle, et de l'avenir', *Revue et Gazette musicale de Paris*, VI, 17, 28 April 1839, p. 129.

3 Quoted in David Blayney Brown, *Romanticism* (London, 2001), p. 63.

4 Reprinted in his collected *Essays in the History of Ideas* (Baltimore, 1948), pp. 228–53.

5 Ibid., p. 252.

6 Marilyn Butler, *Romantics, Rebels and Reactionaries. English Literature and its Background 1760–1830* (Oxford, 1981), p. 1.

7 Michel Florisoone, 'Romantisme et néo-classicisme', *Histoire de l'Art*, vol. III, ed. Jean Babelon (Paris, 1965), p. 867; Kenneth Clark, *The Romantic Rebellion. Romantic versus Classical Art* (London, 1973), p. 19; Maurice Cranston, *The Romantic Movement* (Oxford, 1994), p. 1; Rüdiger Safranski, *Romantik. Eine deutsche Affäre* (Munich, 2007), p. 11; Maurice Bowra, *The Romantic Imagination* (Oxford, 1961), p. 271; Hans-Joachim Schoeps, *Deutsche Geistesgeschichte der Neuzeit*, vol. 3: *Von der Auf-*

klärung zur Romantik (Mainz, 1978), p. 267.

8   Hans Eichner, *'Romantic' and its Cognates: the European History of a Word* (Toronto, 1972), p. 501.

9   *Oxford English Dictionary.*

10 Its history in French dictionaries is best followed through the online resource provided by the ARTFL project of the University of Chicago at http://artfl-project.uchicago.edu/node/17.

11 Eckart Klessmann, *Die deutsche Romantik* (Cologne, 1981), p. 10.

12 René Wellek, 'The Concept of "Romanticism" in Literary History. I. The Term "Romantic" and Its Derivatives', *Comparative Literature*, 1, 1, pp. 3–4.

13 John R. Davis, *The Victorians and Germany* (Oxford, 2007), pp. 47, 59–62.

14 Wellek, 'The Concept of "Romanticism" in Literary History', p. 8.

15 Germaine de Staël, *De l'Allemagne*, 2 vols (Paris, 1968), vol. I, pp. 211–24.

16 Sigrid McLaughlin, 'Russia: Romaničeskij – romantičeskij – romantizm', in Eichner, *'Romantic' and its Cognates*, p. 423.

17 Wellek, 'The Concept of "Romanticism" in Literary History', p. 10.

18 Ibid., p. 12. The quotation by Goethe is to be found in Olga Ragusa, 'Italy: romantico, romanticismo', in Eichner, *'Romantic' and its Cognates*, p. 293. For the spread of the word, see also the helpful chronology in Ibid., pp. 501–12.

19 Quoted in McLaughlin, 'Russia: Romaničeskij – romantičeskij – romantizm', p. 418.

20 Eckart Klessmann, *Die deutsche Romantik*, p. 7.

21 David Watkin and Tilman Mellinghoff, *German Architecture and the Classical Ideal 1740–1840* (London, 1987), p. 178.

22 Blayney Brown, *Romanticism*, p. 8.

23 Christopher Ricks (ed.), *Tennyson. A Selected Edition* (London, 1969), p. 348.

24 I have discussed this in *The Pursuit of Glory: Europe 1648–1815* (London, 2007), ch. 10.

25 Otto Gierke, *Natural Law and the Theory of Society, 1500 to 1800; with a Lecture on The Ideas of Natural Law and Humanity, by Ernst Troeltsch*; translated with an introduction by Ernest Barker (Cambridge, 1934), p. 203.

26 Lytton Strachey, 'The Rousseau affair', in his collected essays *Books and Characters, French and English* (London, 1922), p. 174.

27 P.M.S. Dawson, *The Unacknowledged Legislator. Shelley and Politics* (Oxford, 1980), pp. 263, 269.

Chapter One

1 Lester G. Crocker (ed.), *The Age of Enlightenment* (London, 1969), pp. 291–2.

2 Robert Darnton, *The Business of Enlightenment. A Publishing History of the Encyclopédie 1775–1800* (Cambridge, Mass., 1979), p. 528.

3 Maurice Cranston, *Jean-Jacques. The Early Life and Works of Jean-Jacques Rousseau 1712–1754* (Harmondsworth, 1987), p. 271.

4 Dena Goodman, *The Republic of Letters. A Cultural History of the French Enlightenment* (Ithaca and London, 1994), p. 27.

5   Quoted in Jean Le Rond D'Alembert, *Preliminary Discourse to the Encyclopedia of Diderot*, trans. Richard N. Schwab (New York, 1963), p. xxiv.

6   Jean-Jacques Rousseau, *The Confessions*, ed. J.M. Cohen (London, 1953), p. 327.

7   Maurice Cranston, *Jean-Jacques*, p. 228.

8   Jean-Jacques Rousseau, *Discourse on the Sciences and the Arts*, in Jean-Jacques Rousseau, *The Discourses and Other Early Political Writings*, ed. Victor Gourevich (Cambridge, 1997), pp. 16, 25–6.

9   Arthur M. Wilson, *Diderot* (New York, 1972), p. 181.

10 This episode, which was occasioned by the success at court of Rousseau's opera *Le Devin vu village*, is recounted in T.C.W. Blanning, *The Culture of Power and the Power of Culture. Old Regime Europe, 1660–1789* (Oxford, 2002), pp. 363–4.

11 Ronald C. Rosbottom, 'The novel and gender difference', in Denis Hollier (ed.), *A New History of French Literature* (Cambridge, Mass., and London, 1989), p. 481; Maurice Cranston, *The Noble Savage: Jean-Jacques Rousseau 1754–1762* (London, 1991), p. 263.

12 Robert Darnton, *The Great Cat Massacre and Other Episodes in French Cultural History* (New York, 1984), p. 242.

13 R.A. Leigh (ed.), *Correspondance complète de Jean-Jacques Rousseau*, vol. VIII (Geneva, 1969), p. 292. There are many more such examples in this volume and the following two. For a convenient summary, see Darnton, *The Great Cat Massacre*, pp. 242–3.

14 Ibid., p. 243.

15 Rousseau, *The Confessions*, p. 506.

16 Ibid., p. 17.

17 Plato, *The Republic*, ed. G.R.F. Ferrari, trans. Tom Griffith (Cambridge, 2000), pp. 315–16.

18 Voltaire, *The Age of Louis XIV*, ed. F.C. Green, trans. Martyn P. Pollack (London, 1961), p. 370.

19 Béatrice Didier, *La Musique des lumières. Diderot – L'Encyclopédie – Rousseau* (Paris, 1985), p. 19.

20 David Irwin (ed.), *Winckelmann: Writings on Art* (London, 1972), p. 61.

21 Sir Joshua Reynolds, *Discourses on Art*, ed. Robert R. Wark (London, 1966), p. 19.

22 Peter H. Feist, Thomas Häntzsche, Ulrike Krenzlin and Gisold Lammel, *Geschichte der deutschen Kunst 1760–1848* (Leipzig, 1986), p. 29.

23 Rousseau, *The Confessions*, p. 115.

24 K. Andrews, *The Nazarenes: a Brotherhood of German Painters in Rome* (Oxford, 1964), p. 6.

25 Nikolaus Pevsner, *Academies of Art – Past and Present* (Cambridge, 1940), p. 191.

26 Quoted in Isaiah Berlin, 'The counter-enlightenment', in *idem, Against the Current: Essays in the History of Ideas* (London, 1979), p. 10; Christian Friedrich Daniel Schubart (ed.), *Deutsche Chronik auf das Jahr 1774* (reprinted, Heidelberg, 1975), Erste Beylage zur Deutschen Chronik, August 1774, p. 5.

27 Quoted in Hugh Honour, *Romanticism* (London, 1979), p. 245.

28 By Herbert von Einem, *Deutsche Malerei des Klassizismus und der Romantik 1760–1840* (Munich, 1978), p. 45.

29 William Vaughan, *German Romantic Painting* (New Haven, 1980), p. 33.

30 Quoted in Ibid., p. 45.

31 See below, pp. 64–9

32 Pevsner, *Academies of Art*, p. 192.

33 Rousseau, *The Confessions*, p. 262.

34 G.W. Hegel, *Aesthetics. Lectures on Fine Art*, trans. T.M. Knox, 2 vols (Oxford, 1975), p. 519.

35 These contrasting metaphors provide the title for one of the most important discussions of romantic aesthetics – M.H. Abrams, *The Mirror and the Lamp. Romantic Theory and the Critical Tradition* (Oxford, 1971) [first edition 1953].

36 Quoted in Theodore Besterman, *Voltaire*, 3rd edn (Oxford, 1976), p. 246.

37 Cranston, *Jean-Jacques*, p. 248.

38 Quoted in Lester G. Crocker (ed.), *The Age of Enlightenment*, p. 294.

39 This comment was related to me by the late Robert Wokler but I have not been able to find a source. John Morley in his *Voltaire* (London, 1891), p. 120, wrote: 'his style is like a translucent stream of purest mountain water, moving with swift and animated flow under flashing sunbeams', but that is not quite the same thing.

40 Quoted in Roy Pascal, *The German Sturm und Drang* (Manchester, 1953), p. 88.

41 Quoted in Isaiah Berlin, 'The counter-enlightenment', in idem, *Against the Current*, p. 8.

42 Joachim Maass, *Kleist. Die Geschichte seines Lebens* (Bern and Munich, 1977), p. 70.

43 A.W. Schlegel, 'Über Litteratur, Kunst und Geist des Zeitalters', in Friedrich von Schlegel (ed.), *Europa. Eine Zeitschrift*, vol. II, 1 (1803), p. 82. These were lectures given at Berlin at the end of 1802.

44 Goethe, *Faust*, Part One, trans. David Luke (Oxford, 1987), p. 10.

45 S. Foster Damon, *A Blake Dictionary. The Ideas and Symbols of William Blake* (Providence, 1965), pp. 28, 234.

46 *Collected Letters of Samuel Taylor Coleridge*, ed. Earl Leslie Griggs, vol. I (Oxford, 1956), p. 210.

47 Ibid., vol. II, p. 387.

48 R.R. Palmer, *Catholics and Unbelievers in Eighteenth Century France* (Princeton, 1939), p. 131.

49 Richard Holmes, *The Age of Wonder. How the Romantic Generation Discovered the Beauty and Terror of Science* (London, 2008), pp. xvi–xvii.

50 *Collected Letters of Samuel Taylor Coleridge*, vol. II, p. 387.

51 Quoted in H.S. Reiss (ed.), *The Political Thought of the German Romantics* (Oxford, 1955), p. 137.

52 Quoted in Werner Hofmann, *Caspar David Friedrich* (London, 2000), p. 269.

53 Maurice Cranston, *The Romantic Movement* (Oxford, 1994), p. 53.

54 Johann Wolfgang von Goethe, *The Sufferings of Young Werther*, trans. Bayard Quincy Morgan (London, 1957), pp. 20–2.

55 Ibid., p. 63.

56 Quoted in Marilyn Butler, *Romantics, Rebels and Reactionaries. English Literature and its Background 1760–1830* (Oxford, 1981), p. 168.

57 For a concise summary, see Robert Stern's introduction to Friedrich Wilhelm Joseph von Schelling, *Ideas for a Philosophy of Nature as Introduction to the Study of this Science*, trans. Errol E. Harris and Peter Heath (Cambridge, 1988).

58 Timothy Mitchell, *Art and Science in German Landscape Painting, 1770–1840* (Oxford, 1993), p. 77.

59 Quoted in Ibid., p. 75. See also the acute analysis of Runge's painting in Robert Rosenblum, *The Romantic Child from Runge to Sendak* (London, 1998), pp. 24–9.

60 Robert Rosenblum and H.W. Janson, *Art of the Nineteenth Century. Painting and Sculpture* (London, 1984), p. 87.

61 Cranston, *The Romantic Movement*, p. 38.

62 Jens Christian Jensen, *Caspar David Friedrich. Leben und Werk* , 10th edn (Cologne, 1995), p. 181.

63 William Wordsworth, *The Excursion*, E. de Selincourt and Helen Darbishire (eds), *The Poetical Works of William Wordsworth*, vol. 5 (Oxford, 1949), Book I: *The Wanderer*, pp. 15–16, lines 219–34.

64 Ibid., p.82.

65 Quoted in Vaughan, *German Romantic Painting*, p. 68.

66 Jensen, *Caspar David Friedrich*, p. 210.

67 His friend Georg Friedrich Kersting painted at least three pictures of him at work in his austere studio – Hannelore Gärtner, *Georg Friedrich Kersting* (Leipzig, 1988), illustrations 29, 31, 32.

68 Quoted in Hofmann, *Caspar David Friedrich*, p. 101.

69 von Einem, *Deutsche Malerei*, p. 13.

70 Edward Young, *Conjectures on Original Composition, in a Letter to the Author of Sir Charles Grandison* (London, 1759), p. 26.

71 Ibid., pp. 26–7.

72 Ibid., p. 36.

73 Ibid., p. 28.

74 Abrams, *The Mirror and the Lamp*, p. 199.

75 Isaiah Berlin, *The Magus of the North: J.G. Hamann and*

the Origins of Modern Irrationalism (London, 1993). 'The Magus of the North' was one of the many ironic titles Hamann gave himself.

76 Quoted in W.D. Robson-Scott, *The Literary Background of the Gothic Revival in Germany* (Oxford, 1965), p. 59. It is regrettable that a recent anthology of Hamann's writings, translated into English, should include only the dedications of *Socratic Memorabilia* – Kenneth Haynes (ed.), *Hamann: Writings on Philosophy and Language* (Cambridge, 2007).

77 Nicholas Boyle, *Goethe. The Poet and the Age*, vol. 1: *The poetry of desire* (Oxford, 1991), p. 38.

78 Johann Wolfgang von Goethe, *Dichtung und Wahrheit*, Part 3, Book 12 (Munich, 1962), pp. 64–6.

79 Johann Wolfgang von Goethe, 'Von deutscher Baukunst', in Johann Gottfried Herder (ed.), *Von deutscher Art und Kunst* (1773), ed. Edna Purdie (Oxford, 1924), p. 129.

80 Paul Frankl, *The Gothic. Literary Sources and Interpretations through Eight Centuries* (Princeton, 1960), p. 417.

81 Carl Hammer, *Goethe and Rousseau. Resonances of the mind* (Lexington, 1973), pp. 36–7; Eugene L. Stelzig, *The Romantic Subject in Autobiography: Rousseau and Goethe* (Charlottesville and London, 2000), pp. 138–9.

82 Jean-Jacques Rousseau, *A Complete Dictionary of Music, consisting of a copious Explanation of all Words necessary to a true Knowledge and Understanding of Music*, trans. William Waring, 2nd edn (London, 1779), p. 182.

83 All these and other tributes are to be found in Raymond Trousson, 'Jean-Jacques Rousseau et son œuvre dans la presse périodique allemande de 1750 à 1800', *Dix-huitième Siècle*, 1 (1969), pp. 289–90.

84 Herbert Dieckmann, 'Diderot's Conception of Genius', *Journal of the History of Ideas*, 2, 2 (1941), p. 152.

85 John Brewer, '"The most polite age and the most vicious". Attitudes towards culture as a commodity 1660–1800', in Ann Bermingham and John Brewer (eds), *The Consumption of Culture 1600–1800. Image, Object, Text* (London and New York, 1995), p. 350. Samuel Johnson, *A dictionary of the English language : in which the words are deduced from their originals : and illustrated in their different significations by examples from the best writers : to which are prefixed, a history of the language, and an English grammar*, vol. I (London, 1755), unpaginated.

86 L.D. Ettlinger, *'Winckelmann'*, *The age of neo-classicism*, The fourteenth exhibition of the Council of Europe (London, 1972), pp. xxxiii–iv.

87 Michael Forsyth, *Buildings for Music. The Architect, the Musician, and the Listener from the Seventeenth Century to the Present Day* (Cambridge, Mass., 1985), p. 104.

88 Quoted in Adolf Rosenberg, 'Friedrich der Große als Kunstsammler', *Zeitschrift für bildende Kunst*, new series, 4 (1893), p. 209.

89 Quoted in James J. Sheehan, *Museums in the German Art World. From the End of the Old Regime to the Rise of Modernism* (New York, 2000), p. 26.

90 Frances Burney, *Evelina, or The History of a Young Lady's Entrance into the World*, ed. Margaret Anne Doody (London, 1994), p. 116.

91 Wilhelm Heinrich Wackenroder and Ludwig Tieck, *Herzensergießungen eines kunstliebenden Klosterbruders*, ed. A. Gillies (Oxford, 1966), p. 92.

92 James H. Johnson, *Listening in Paris. A Cultural History*

(Berkeley and Los Angeles, 1995), p. 269.

93 Ibid., p. 259.

94 Gerhard von Breuning, *Memories of Beethoven. From the House of the Black-Robed Spaniards*, ed. Maynard Solomon (Cambridge, 1992), pp. 109–10.

95 Ibid., p. 111. Cf. Christopher H. Gibbs, 'Performances of grief: Vienna's response to the death of Beethoven', in Scott Burnham and Michael P. Steinberg (eds), *Beethoven and his World* (Princeton, 2000), p. 251.

96 Quoted in Paul Johnson, *The Birth of the Modern: World Society, 1815–1830* (London, 1991), p. 117.

97 Richard Wagner, *My Life* (Cambridge, 1983), p. 30.

98 Quoted in Alan Walker, *Franz Liszt. The Virtuoso Years, 1811–1847*, revised edn (London, 1989), p. 417.

99 There is a good – and very entertaining – account in Ibid., pp. 417–26.

100 Franz Liszt, 'De la situation des artistes et de leur condition dans la société', *Gazette musicale de Paris*, II, 19, 10 May 1835; 20, 17 May 1835; 30, 26 July 1835; 35, 30 August 1835; 41, 11 October 1835.

101 Adrian Williams (ed.), *Portrait of Liszt by Himself and his Contemporaries* (Oxford, 1990), p. 351.

102 In a letter to the members of the musical association on the island of Rügen – H.C. Robbins Landon, *Haydn: Chronicle and Works*, vol. V: *Haydn: the Late Years* (London, 1977), p. 233.

103 *The Musical World*, XIX, 36, 5 September 1844, p. 291; Williams (ed.), *Portrait of Liszt*, p. 224.

104 *The Works of Elizabeth Barrett Browning*, ed. Karen Hill (Ware, 1994), p. 329.

105 Howard Erskine-Hill, 'Pope, Alexander (1688–1744)',

Oxford Dictionary of National Biography, Oxford University Press, Sept 2004; online edn, Jan. 2008 [http://www.oxforddnb.com/view/article/22526, accessed 30 Sept. 2008]

106 Volkmar Braunbehrens, *Mozart in Vienna* (Oxford, 1991), pp. 316, 331, 349, 363, 368, 419–21.

107 Quoted in K.M. Baker, 'Politique et opinion publique sous l'ancien régime', *Annales. Économie, Société, Civilisation*, 42, 1 (1987), pp. 56–7.

108 Cyril Ehrlich, *The Piano. A History*, revised edn (Oxford, 1990), p. 17.

109 Klaus Lankheit, *Revolution und Restauration 1785–1855* (Cologne, 1988), p. 9.

110 *Allgemeine Musikalische Zeitung*, XXIV, 1 (2 January 1822), p. 1.

111 Quoted in Jochen Schulte-Sasse, 'Kritisch rationale und literarische Öffentlichkeit', *Aufklärung und literarische Öffentlichkeit*, eds Christa Bürger, Peter Bürger and Jochen Schulte-Sasse (Frankfurt am Main, 1980), p. 30.

112 Williams (ed.), *Portrait of Liszt*, p. 581.

113 L.A. Willoughby, 'Classic and romantic: a re-examination', *German Life and Letters*, 6 (1952), p. 5.

114 Quoted in H. Kiesel and P. Münch, *Gesellschaft und Literatur im 18. Jahrhundert* (Munich, 1977), p. 98.

115 Nicholas Cook, *Music: a Very Short Introduction* (Oxford, 1998), p. 28; Elliot Forbes (ed.), *Thayer's Life of Beethoven*, revised edn (Princeton, 1969), p. 1046; Stephen Rumph, *Beethoven after Napoleon. Political Romanticism in the Late Works* (Berkeley, Los Angeles and London, 2004), p. 195.

116 Quoted in William Weber, 'Wagner, Wagnerism and musical idealism', in David C. Large and William Weber (eds), *Wagnerism in European Culture and Politics* (Ithaca and London, 1984), p. 44.

117 Johann Wolfgang von Goethe, Review of Johann Georg Sulzer, *Allgemeine Theorie der schönen Künste in einzelnen, nach alphabetischer Ordnung der Kunstwörter, auf einander folgenden Artikeln* (Leipzig, 1771), first published in the *Frankfurter gelehrten Anzeigen* (1772), here in *Goethes Werke*, hrsg. im Auftrage der Großherzogin Sophie von Sachsen, vol. 37 (Weimar, 1896), p. 213.

118 Raymond Williams, *Culture and Society 1780–1950* (London, 1958), pp. 33, 35.

119 Quoted in Rüdiger Safranski, *Romantik. Eine deutsche Affäre* (Munich, 2007), pp. 106–7.

120 Dieter Arendt, 'Brentanos Philister-Rede am Ende des romantischen Jahrhunderts oder Der Philister-Krieg und seine unrühmliche Kapitulation', *Orbis Litterarum*, 55, 2 (2000).

121 Quoted in F.W.J. Hemmings, *Culture and Society in France 1789–1848* (Leicester, 1987), p. 260.

122 T.J. Reed, *Schiller* (Oxford, 1991), pp. 68–9.

123 James J. Sheehan, *German History, 1770–1866* (Oxford, 1989), p. 329.

124 Book 5, chapter 2. Eric Blackall (ed.), *Goethe: The Collected Works*, vol. 9: *Wilhelm Meister's Apprenticeship* (Princeton, 1995), p. 172.

125 Goethe, *Faust*, Part One, p. 20.

126 Johann Peter Eckermann, *Gespräche mit Goethe in den letzten Jahren seines Lebens 1823–1832*, ed. Ernst Merian-Genast, 2 vols (Basle, 1945), vol. I, p. 309.

127 Goethe, *Faust*, Part Two, trans. David Luke (Oxford, 1994), p. 223.

128 Mack Walker, *German Home Towns* (Ithaca, 1971), pp. 29–33.

129 Albert Cassagne, *La Théorie de l'art pour l'art en France chez les derniers romantiques et les premiers réalistes* (Paris, 1906), p. 23.

130 Benjamin Constant, *Journal intime, précédé du Cahier rouge et d'Adolphe*, ed. Jean Mistler (Monaco, 1945), p. 159. 'J'ai une conversation avec Robinson, élève de Schelling. Son travail sur *l'Ésthetique* de Kant a des idées très énergiques. L'art pour l'art, sans but, car tout but dénature l'art'. In *Modern Language Notes* for March 1910, J.E. Spingarn correctly identified Constant's use of the phrase in his *Journal intime* but simply stated, 'Constant sums up Schelling's aesthetics' without mentioning Robinson's intermediary role.

131 Ibid., pp. 38–9; Alfred Michiels, *Histoire des idées littéraires en France au XIXe siècle*, vol. II (Paris, 1863), p. 113.

132 Cassagne, *La Théorie de l'art pour l'art*, p. 53.

133 Stendhal, *Life of Rossini*, trans. Richard N. Coe (London, 1956), pp. 235, 371, 407–8.

134 Joseph d'Ortigue, 'Des sociétés philharmoniques dans le Midi de la France', *Gazette musicale de Paris*, I, 48, 30 November 1824, p. 383.

135 *Revue et Gazette musicale de Paris*, II, no. 46 (15 November 1835).

136 Walker, *Franz Liszt. The Virtuoso Years*, p. 250.

137 A. Specht, 'Vocabulaire artistique: le bourgeois', *Revue et Gazette Musical de Paris*, X, 53 (31 December 1843), pp. 440–2.

138 Alexander Pope, *Essay on Man*, i, 289–94.

139 Alexander Pope, *Imitations of Horace*, *The Poems of Alexander Pope*, ed. John Butt, vol. IV, 2nd edn (London and New Haven, 1953), p. 187.

140 Besterman, *Voltaire*, pp. 367–72.

141 Voltaire, *Candide*, trans. Norman Cameron (London, 1947), pp. 13–14.

142 Indeed, Rousseau wrote to Voltaire to criticise his treatment of the Lisbon earthquake – Nicholas Shrady, *The Last Day: Wrath, Ruin and Reason in the Great Lisbon Earthquake of 1755* (New York, 2008), pp. 122–3.

143 Peter Gay, *The Enlightenment: an Interpretation*, vol. 2: *The Science of Freedom* (New York, 1969), p. 531. Although he writes with his customary fluency and intelligence about Rousseau, Gay overestimates Rousseau's enlightened characteristics.

144 David Edmonds and John Eidinow, *Rousseau's Dog. Two Great Thinkers at War in the Age of Enlightenment* (London, 2006), p. 163. As this highly entertaining account reveals, both men behaved badly but it was Rousseau's paranoia that was to blame for the rupture.

145 Rousseau, *The Confessions*, p. 190.

146 Hyder Edward Rollins (ed.), *The Letters of John Keats 1814–21*, 2 vols (Cambridge, 1958), vol. I, p. 184.

147 G.L. Strachey, *Landmarks in French Literature* (London, n.d.), pp. 184–6, 189.

Chapter Two

1 'Ode to a Nightingale', Miriam Allott (ed.), *The Poems of John Keats* (London, 1970), p. 529.

2   James E. May, 'Young, Edward (*bap.* 1683, *d.* 1765)', *Oxford Dictionary of National Biography*, Oxford University Press, 2004 [http://www.oxforddnb.com/view/article/30260, accessed 16 Oct. 2008].

3   Quoted in W.D. Robson-Scott, *The Literary Background of the Gothic Revival in Germany* (Oxford, 1965), pp. 37–8.

4   John Louis Kind, *Edward Young in Germany* (New York, 1906), p. 41.

5   Ibid., p. 29.

6   H.S. Reiss (ed.), *The Political Thought of the German Romantics* (Oxford, 1955), p. 134.

7   Quoted in Maurice Bowra, *The Romantic Imagination* (Oxford, 1961), p. 4.

8   Etymologically there is no link between the 'mare' of 'nightmare' and a female horse but the two were often compounded.

9   Ernst Beutler, 'Johann Heinrich Füssli', *Goethe. Viermonatsschrift der Goethe-Gesellschaft*, 4 (1939), p. 19.

10 Ibid; H.W. Janson, *Sixteen Studies* (New York, 1973), p. 79. This chapter entitled 'Fuseli's Nightmare' appeared originally in *Arts and Sciences*, II, 1 (1963).

11 Ibid., p. 82. The first of these quotations can also be found in Nicolas Powell, *Fuseli, 'The Nightmare'* (London, 1973), p. 60. Powell is at pains to stress the traditional elements in Fuseli's work, stating firmly: 'To regard this picture [*The Nightmare*] as a precocious example of nineteenth-century romanticism, let alone of Surrealism, is to misunderstand it', but he both underestimates the originality of Fuseli's vision and imposes too demanding a definition of romanticism. More cogent is Michael Levey's conclusion: 'the individual's sensations are what matter; and

in opting out of the social framework, Fuseli is already romantic' – *Rococo to Revolution: Major Trends in Eighteenth-Century Painting* (London, 1966), p. 202.

12 Janson, *Sixteen Studies*, p. 79.

13 Karl S. Guthke, 'Introduction', Henry Fuseli, *Remarks on the Writing and Conduct of J.J. Rousseau*, reprinted in facsimile (Los Angeles, 1960), p. ii; Eudo C. Mason, *The Mind of Henry Fuseli. Selections from his Writings with an Introductory Study* (London, 1951), pp. 13, 43–4.

14 Mason, *The Mind of Henry Fuseli*, p. 67.

15 Ibid., p. 69.

16 It is reproduced in Martin Myrone, *Henry Fuseli* (London, 2001), p. 14.

17 *Henry Fuseli 1741–1825* (London, 1975), p. 39; Michael Levey, *Rococo to Revolution*, p. 201.

18 Christoph Becker, 'Friar Puck und Fairy-shot. Geister in Füsslis Kunst', in Franziska Lentzsch (ed.), *Füssli: the Wild Swiss* (Zürich, 2005), pp. 115–42. This exhibition catalogue contains a host of excellent reproductions of Fuseli's work.

19 Heinrich Fuessli, *Aphorismen über die Kunst* (Basle, 1944), p. 132.

20 Second ode on Art [between 1772 and 1775]:
> Among the mob that every rotten wind
> Blows into your palaces, O Rome,
> The mob of Germans, Britons, French,
> The mob of Polish and of Muscovites
> The vermin of art – thus I spent a day
> Wandering with trembling foot among your temples
> And cursed in furor incessate
> The academies of London and of France.

A.M. Atkins, '"Both Turk and Jew": notes on the poetry of

Henry Fuseli, with some translations', *Blake: An Illustrated Quarterly*, 16, 4 (1983), p. 209. Fuseli's aversion to academic art did not prevent him enjoying a mutually beneficial relationship with the Royal Academy in London.

21 Perhaps not surprisingly this has been reproduced many times. A high-quality reproduction, together with another similar scene, can be found in Rolf Toman (ed.), *Klassizismus und Romantik. Architektur – Skulptur – Malerei – Zeichnung. 1750–1848* (Cologne, 2000), p. 341.

22 Quoted in David Blayney Brown, *Romanticism* (London, 2001), p. 316.

23 Quoted in Myrone, *Henry Fuseli*, pp. 46–7.

24 Ibid.

25 Jean-Jacques Rousseau, *The Confessions*, ed. J.M. Cohen (London, 1953), pp. 27–8.

26 Ibid., p. 408.

27 Friedrich Schlegel, *Lucinde and the Fragments*, ed. Peter Virchow (Minneapolis, 1971), p. 44.

28 Quoted in Maurice Cranston, *The Romantic Movement* (Oxford, 1994), p. 35.

29 Rüdiger Safranski, *Romantik. Eine deutsche Affäre* (Munich, 2007), p. 13.

30 Eckart Klessmann, *Die deutsche Romantik* (Cologne, 1981), p. 167.

31 Werner Hofmann, *Caspar David Friedrich* (London, 2000), pp. 86, 89–91, 152–3, 158–9, 164–5, 168–9, 173–5, 179, 194, 196–7, 233, 246–9.

32 Jens Christian Jensen, *Caspar David Friedrich. Leben und Werk* , 10th edn (Cologne, 1995), p. 228.

33 James Knowlson, *Damned to Fame. The Life of Samuel Beckett* (New York, 1996), p. 342. A recent poll of 800

playwrights, actors, directors and journalists conducted by the National Theatre voted *Waiting for Godot* 'the most significant English-language play of the twentieth century', notwithstanding the fact that the first version was written in French – http://www.samuel-beckett.net/ BerlinTraffic.html.

34 Nicholas Temperley, 'John Field and the first nocturne', *Music and Letters*, 56 (1975), p. 337.

35 Robin Langley, 'Field, John', *Grove Music Online. Oxford Music Online.* 2 Dec. 2008, http://www.oxfordmusiconline.com/subscriber/article/ grove/music/09603; Michael Cole, *The Pianoforte in the Classical Era* (Oxford, 1998), p. 107.

36 Franz Liszt, 'John Field und seine Nocturnes (1859)', in Franz Liszt, *Gesammelte Schriften*, ed. L. Ramann, 6 vols. (Leipzig, 1880–3), vol. IV, p. 268. Although Liszt writes with feeling and insight about Field and his music, his biographical section begins: 'Born in England, at Dublin in 1782 . . .'

37 Steven Lebetter, untitled introduction to the recording of Field's nocturnes by John O'Connor – Telarc CD-80199.

38 Otto Erich Deutsch (ed.), *Schubert. Memoirs by his Friends* (London, 1958), p. 138.

39 Quoted in Paul Lawley, '"The grim journey": Beckett Listens to Schubert', in Angela Moorjani and Carola Veit (eds), *Samuel Beckett: Endlessness in the Year 2000 = Samuel Beckett: fin sans fin en l'an 2000* (Amsterdam, 2001), p. 260.

40 The best-quality reproductions of the three versions are to be found in Werner Hofmann, *Das entzweite Jahrhundert. Kunst zwischen 1750 und 1830* (Munich, 1995), pp. 541–3.

41 Quoted in Alfonso E. Pérez Sánchez and Eleanor A.

Sayre (eds), *Goya and the Spirit of Enlightenment* (Boston, 1989), p. 115.

42 Ibid., p. 111.

43 Ibid., p. 115.

44 Robert Hughes, *Goya* (London, 2003), pp. 165–7.

45 Priscilla E. Muller, 'Goya, Francisco de,' in *Grove Art Online. Oxford Art Online*, http://www.oxfordart online.com/subscriber/article/grove/art/T033882 (accessed 9 Dec. 2008).

46 Hughes, *Goya*, pp. 127–8.

47 Ibid., pp. 130–1; Hofmann, *Das entzweite Jahrhundert*, p. 516.

48 Hughes, *Goya*, p. 140.

49 Nigel Glendinning, *Goya and his Critics* (New Haven and London, 1977), pp. 45–6. Glendinning quotes this and subsequent documents in full.

50 Ibid., p. 49.

51 Ludwig Achim von Arnim and Clemens Brentano, *Des Knaben Wunderhorn*, 3 vols. (Munich, 1963), p. 861.

52 See above, p. 57.

53 There is a small reproduction in Hughes, *Goya*, p. 192. For a much larger version, see Camilo José Cela, *Los Caprichos de Francisco de Goya y Lucientes* (Madrid, 1989), p. 51.

54 Blayney Brown, *Romanticism*, p. 316.

55 Quoted in André Malraux, *Saturn. An Essay on Goya* (London, 1957), p. 25.

56 Quoted in José López-Rey, *Goya's Caprichos*, vol. I (Princeton, 1953), p. 102.

57 Goethe, *Faust*, Part One, trans. David Luke (Oxford, 1987), pp. 130–1.

58 Ibid., p. 131.

59 Allott (ed.), *The Poems of John Keats*, p. 539. For an illu-
   minating analysis of this and other poems by Keats, see
   Robin Mayhead, *John Keats* (Cambridge, 1967), *passim*.

60 Allott (ed.), *The Poems of John Keats*, p. 525.

61 Ibid., p. 527.

62 Alethea Hayter, 'Introduction', in Thomas De Quincey,
   Confessions of an English Opium Eater, ed. Alethea Hayter
   (Oxford, 1971), p. 14.

63 Ibid., pp. 20, 48.

64 David Cairns, *Berlioz*, vol. I: *The Making of an Artist,
   1803–1832* (London, 1989), pp. 329–30.

65 David Cairns (ed.), *The Memoirs of Hector Berlioz*
   (London, 1969), p. 576.

66 Cairns, *Berlioz*, I, p. 339.

67 Ibid., p. 332. Cf. Nicholas Temperley, 'The "Symphonie
   fantastique" and its programme', *The Musical Quarterly*,
   57, 4 (1971), pp. 593–608.

68 Cairns, *Berlioz*, I, pp. 327–8.

69 Ibid., pp. 328–9.

70 Hugh Macdonald, 'Berlioz, Hector,' in *Grove Music
   Online. Oxford Music Online*, http://www.oxfordmusic
   online.com/subscriber/article/grove/music/51424pg14
   (accessed 12 Dec. 2008).

71 'Concert dramatique de M. Berlioz', *Revue Musicale*, VI,
   46 (15 December 1832), pp. 365–6.

72 Édouard Fétis, 'Concert donné par M. Berlioz', Ibid.,
   VIII, 48 (30 November 1834), p. 381. Almost exactly the
   same criticism was made 170 years later by Rodney Milnes
   in an article in *BBC Music Magazine*, in which Berlioz's
   music was dismissed as unbearably long-winded, utterly
   humourless, devoid of any sense of stage time, and incap-

able of sustaining a melodic argument – http://find articles.com/p/articles/mi_qa3724/is_200401/ai_ n9359319.

73 'Aus dem Leben eines Künstlers', *Neue Zeitschrift für Musik*, III (1835), 3, 1 (3 July 1835), p. 1.

74 These are two of four epigraphs provided by Frederick Burwick for his *Poetic Madness and the Romantic Imagination* (University Park, Pa., 1996), p. 1.

75 *Absalom and Achitophel*, lines 163–4.

76 Roy Porter, *Mind-forg'd Manacles. A History of Madness in England from the Restoration to the Regency* (London, 1987), p. 10.

77 Roy Porter, 'Mood disorders: social section', in German E. Berrios and Roy Porter (eds), *A History of Clinical Psychiatry. The Origin and History of Psychiatric Disorders* (London, 1995), p. 418.

78 Sander Gilman, *Seeing the Insane* (New York, 1982), p. 126. Gilman gives many other examples from the period.

79 Ibid., pp. 84–9.

80 Daniel Berthold-Bond, *Hegel's Theory of Madness* (Albany, NY, 1995), pp. 1–3, 14, 26–7.

81 George MacLennan, *Lucid Interval: Subjective Writing and Madness in History* (Leicester, 1992), p. 78.

82 Quoted in Charles Rosen, *The Romantic Generation* (New York, 1996), p. 646.

83 Ibid., p. 647.

84 Ellen Rosand, 'Operatic madness: a challenge to convention', in Steven Paul Scher (ed.), *Music and Text: Critical Inquiries* (Cambridge, 1992), p. 287.

85 Stephen A. Willier, 'Mad scene', *The New Grove Dictionary of Opera*, ed. Stanley Sadie. *Grove Music Online.*

Oxford Music Online. 7 Jan. 2009, http://www.oxford
musiconline.com/subscriber/article/grove/music/
O007756; Sieghart Döhring, 'Die Wahnsinnszene', in
Heinz Becker (ed.), *Die 'couleur locale' in der Oper des 19.
Jahrhunderts* (Regensburg, 1976), pp. 282–5.

86 Deutsche Grammophon DVD 00440 073 4109.

87 Enid Peschel and Richard Peschel, 'Donizetti and the
music of mental derangement: *Anna Bolena, Lucia di Lammermoor,* and the composer's neurobiological illness', *The
Yale Journal of Biology and Medicine,* 65 (1992), pp. 189,
192. Cf. A. Erfurth and P. Hoff, 'Mad scenes in early
nineteenth-century opera', *Acta Psychiatrica Scandinavica,*
102 (2000), pp. 310–13.

88 Marion Kant (ed.), *The Cambridge Companion to Ballet*
(Cambridge, 2008), p. 184.

89 Johann Wolfgang von Goethe, *Götz von Berlichingen,
Goethes Werke,* ed. Erich Trunz, 14 vols (Munich, 1981),
Dramatische Dichtungen, vol. II, p. 175.

90 Ibid., p. 101.

91 *Über die deutsche Literatur; die Mängel, die man ihr
vorwerfen kann; die Ursachen derselben und die Mittel, sie
zu verbessern,* reprinted in Horst Steinmetz (ed.), *Friedrich
II, König von Preußen und die deutsche Literatur des 18.
Jahrhunderts. Texte und Dokumente* (Stuttgart, 1985), pp.
81–2.

92 For a good sample of contemporary responses, see Kurt
Rothmann, *Johann Wolfgang von Goethe, Die Leiden des
jungen Werthers: Erläuterungen und Dokumente* (Stuttgart,
1987), pp. 130–50.

93 Christian Friedrich Daniel Schubart (ed.), *Deutsche
Chronik,* I (1774), p. 574.

94 Nicholas Boyle, *Goethe. The Poet and the Age*, vol. 1: *The Poetry of Desire* (Oxford, 1991), p. 175; Hans-G. Winter, 'Antiklassizismus: Sturm und Drang', in Viktor Zmegac (ed.), *Geschichte der deutschen Literatur vom 18. Jahrhundert bis zur Gegenwart*, vol 1, pt. 1, 2nd edn (Königstein im Taunus, 1984), p. 228.

95 Angelika Müller-Scherf, *Lotte und Werther auf Meißner Porzellan im Zeitalter der Empfindsamkeit* (Wetzlar, 2009).

96 *Eroica*, Opus Arte DVD OA 0908 D.

97 This has been reprinted many times, for example in H.C. Robbins Landon, *Beethoven. A Documentary Study* (London, 1975), p. 86.

98 Paul Johnson, *The Birth of the Modern. World society 1815–1830* (London, 1991), p. 125.

99 Richard Wagner, *My Life* (Cambridge, 1983), p. 30.

100 David Charlton (ed.), *E.T.A. Hoffmann's Musical Writings: Kreisleriana, The Poet and the Composer, Music Criticism* (Cambridge, 1989), pp. 238–9.

101 Ibid., p. 96.

102 Ibid., p. 236.

103 'Charismatic leadership is born of crisis. It has no permanence unless crisis, war and disturbance become normal in society', Norbert Elias, *The Court Society* (Oxford, 1983), p. 121

104 Stendhal, *Life of Rossini*, trans. Richard N. Coe (London, 1956), p. 1.

105 Johnson, *The Birth of the Modern*, p. 126.

106 Alan Walker, *Franz Liszt. The Virtuoso Years 1811–1847*, revised edn (London, 1989), p. 168.

107 Joseph-Marc Bailbé, *La Musique en France à l'époque romantique (1830–1870)* (Paris, 1991), p. 203.

108 Quoted in Ibid., p. 202.

109 Adrian Williams (ed.), *Portrait of Liszt by Himself and his Contemporaries* (Oxford, 1990), p. 41.

110 Ibid., p. 146.

111 Walker, *Franz Liszt. The Virtuoso Years 1811–1847*, revised edn, p. 374.

112 Ibid., p. 287.

113 Ibid., p. 149.

114 Adrian Williams (ed.), *Franz Liszt. Selected letters* (Oxford, 1998), p. 96.

115 Ibid., p. 105.

116 Ibid., p. 141.

117 Fiona MacCarthy, *Byron. Life and Legend* (London, 2003), pp. vii–x.

118 Ibid., p. ix.

Chapter Three

1 Johann Wolfgang von Goethe, *The Sufferings of Young Werther*, trans. Bayard Quincy Morgan (London, 1957), p. 151.

2 Ibid., p. 21.

3 Jens Christian Jensen, *Caspar David Friedrich. Leben und Werk* , 10th edn (Cologne, 1995), p. 114.

4 Robin Buss, *Vigny: Chatterton* (London, 1984), p. 12. It has been argued by Chatterton's most recent biographer that his death was not suicide at all but accidental, the result of mixing arsenic, which he was taking to control his venereal disaease, and opium, which he took for pleasure — Nick Groom, 'Chatterton, Thomas (1752–1770)', *Oxford Dictionary of National Biography*,

Oxford University Press, 2004. [http://www.oxford
dnb.com/view/article/5189, accessed 29 June 2009].

5 Theo Stammen, 'Goethe und das deutsche National-
   albewußtsein im beginnenden 19. Jahrhundert', in Klaus
   Weigelt (ed.), *Heimat und Nation. Zur Geschichte und Iden-
   tität* (Mainz, 1984), p. 119. See also above, p. 34.

6 Johann Wolfgang von Goethe, *Aus meinem Leben. Dichtung und Wahrheit* (Munich, 1962), Part II, Book 9, p. 160.

7 W.D. Robson-Scott, *The Literary Background of the Gothic
   Revival in Germany* (Oxford, 1965), p. 92.

8 Elie Kedourie, *Nationalism*, 4th edn (Oxford, 1993), p. 57.

9 F. M. Barnard, *Herder's Social and Political Thought. From
   Enlightenment to Nationalism* (Oxford, 1965), pp. 56–7.

10 Ibid., p. 57.

11 Quoted in Reinhold Ergang, *Herder and the Foundations
   of German Nationalism* (New York, 1931), p. 105.

12 Sir Walter Scott, *The Antiquary*, ed. Nicola J. Watson
   (Oxford, 2002), p. 3.

13 Sir Walter Scott, *Old Mortality*, ed. Jane Stevenson and
   Peter Davidson (Oxford, 1993), p. xxix.

14 Quoted in Hans-G. Winter, 'Antiklassizismus: Sturm und
   Drang', in Viktor Zmegac (ed.), *Geschichte der deutschen
   Literatur vom 18. Jahrhundert bis zur Gegenwart*, vol. 1, pt.
   1, 2nd edn (Königstein im Taunus, 1984), p. 204.

15 Quoted in Ergang, *Herder*, pp. 153–4.

16 Isaiah Berlin, 'Herder and the Enlightenment', in Earl R.
   Wasserman (ed.), *Aspects of the Eighteenth Century*
   (Baltimore and London, 1965), p. 54.

17 Ergang, *Herder*, pp. 152–3.

18 Louis Réau, *L'Europe française au siècle des lumières* (Paris,
   1951), p. 13.

19 Nicole Ferrier-Caverivière, *L'Image de Louis XIV dans la littérature française de 1660 à 1715* (Paris, 1981), p. 371 n. 71.

20 Quoted in Adrien Fauchier-Magnan, *The Small German Courts in the Eighteenth Century* (London, 1958), p. 27.

21 *Des mœurs, des coutumes, de l'industrie, des progrès de l'esprit humain dans les arts et dans les sciences, Oeuvres de Frédéric le Grand*, 30 vols (Berlin, 1846–56), I, p. 232.

22 Quoted in Rudolf Haym, *Herder nach seinem Leben und seinen Werken*, 2 vols (Berlin, 1880, 1885), vol. I, p. 338.

23 Johann Gottfried Herder, 'Journal meiner Reise im Jahr 1769', *Sämmtliche Werke*, vol. IV, p. 435.

24 Ergang, *Herder*, p. 154

25 Ibid., p. 113.

26 Éléazar de Mauvillon, *Lettres Françoises et Germaniques. Ou reflexions militaires, littéraires, et critiques sur les François et les Allemans. Ouvrage également utile aux officiers & aux beaux-esprits de l'une & de l'autre nation* (London, 1740), pp. 247, 249, 303, 314, 336–7, 345, 349, 357, 365.

27 *Journal de musique, par une société d'amateurs*, continuation of *Journal de musique historique, théorique et pratique, sur la musique ancienne et moderne, les musiciens et les instrumens de tous les temps et de tous les peuples* (reprinted Geneva, 1972), p. 5; Antoine de Rivarol, 'De l'universalité de la langue française', in *Œuvres choisies*, ed. M. de Lescure, 2 vols (Paris, 1880), I, pp. 1–2.

28 Quoted in Patrice L.-R. Higonnet, 'The politics of linguistic terrorism and grammatical hegemony during the French Revolution', *Social History*, 5, 1 (1980), p. 51.

29 Quoted in Maryon McDonald, *'We are not French!' Language, Culture and Identity in Brittany* (London, 1989), p. 32.

30   Quoted in Higonnet, 'The politics of linguistic terrorism', p. 57.

31   Quoted in Denis Woronoff, *La République bourgeoise de Thermidor à Brumaire 1794–1799* (Paris, 1971), p. 159.

32   R.R. Palmer, *Twelve Who Ruled. The Year of the Terror in the French Revolution* (Princeton, 1970), p. 320.

33   Johann Gottlieb Fichte, *Addresses to the German Nation*, edited with an introduction and notes by Gregory Moore (Cambridge, 2008), p. xi.

34   Hagen Schulze, *The Course of German Nationalism. From Frederick the Great to Bismarck 1763–1867* (Cambridge, 1991), p. 111.

35   Fichte, *Addresses to the German Nation*, p. 49.

36   Ibid., p. 58.

37   Ibid., p. 195.

38   Ibid., p. xix.

39   Ibid, p. 88.

40   Roy Pascal, *The German Sturm und Drang* (Manchester, 1953), p. 78.

41   Ergang, *Herder and the Foundations of German Nationalism*, p. 198.

42   Hans Kohn, *The Mind of Germany: the Education of a Nation* (London, 1965), p. 56.

43   Thomas Percy, *Reliques of Ancient English Poetry, consisting of Old Heroic Ballads, Songs, and other Pieces of our Earlier Poets (chiefly of the Lyric kind), together with some few of the later date*, reprinted *in facsimile* with an introduction by Nick Groom (London, 1996), 3 vols, I, pp. ix–x.

44   Pascal, *The German Sturm und Drang*, p. 81.

45   Quoted in Peter Burke, *Popular Culture in Early Modern Europe* (London, 1978), p. 4.

46 Nicholas Boyle, *Goethe. The Poet and the Age*, vol. 1: *The Poetry of Desire* (Oxford, 1991), p. 113. This is the translation offered by Boyle.

47 Annalies Grasshoff, 'Die Literatur der russischen Aufklärung der sechziger bis achtziger Jahre', in Helmut Grasshoff (ed.), *Geschichte der russischen Literatur von den Anfängen bis 1917*, 2 vols (Berlin, 1986), I, p. 180.

48 Rudolf Neuhäuser, *Towards the Romantic Age. Essays on Pre-Romantic and Sentimental Literature in Russia* (The Hague, 1974), p. 138.

49 John Mersereau Jr., 'The nineteenth century: romanticism', in Charles A. Moser (ed.), *The Cambridge History of Russian Literature* (Cambridge, 1989), p. 150.

50 Rüdiger Safranski, *Romantik. Eine deutsche Affäre* (Munich, 2007), p. 182.

51 Ludwig Achim von Arnim and Clemens Brentano, *Des Knaben Wunderhorn*, 3 vols (Munich, 1963), III, pp. 75–5.

52 http://www.recmusic.org/lieder/w/wunderhorn/. Not all of these composers were in any sense romantic, of course.

53 John Warrack, *Carl Maria von Weber*, 2nd edn (Cambridge, 1976), p. 369.

54 'Feuilleton. Carl Maria von Weber und das deutsche Volkslied', Gustav Bock (ed.), *Neue Berliner Musikzeitung*, (1851), IV, no. 27 (3 July 1850), p. 213.

55 Ibid., p. 253.

56 Richard Wagner, *Sämtliche Schriften und Dichtungen*, 5th edn, 12 vols (Leipzig, n.d.), I, p. 220.

57 John O. Hayden (ed.), *William Wordsworth. Selected Prose* (Harmondsworth, 1988), pp. 281–2.

58 David Daiches, *Robert Burns* (London, 1966), p. 308.

59 Donald Sassoon, *The Culture of the Europeans from 1800 to the Present* (London, 2006), p. 146.

60 Fiona Stafford, 'Scottish romanticism and Scotland in romanticism', in Michael Ferber (ed.), *A Companion to European Romanticism* (Oxford, 2005), p. 59; Paul Johnson, *The Birth of the Modern. World Society 1815–1830* (London, 1991), p. 426.

61 Walter Scott, *Waverley*, ed. Claire Lamont (Oxford, 1986), p. xxiii.

62 Maurice Cranston, *The Romantic Movement* (Oxford, 1994), p. 90.

63 Stendhal, *The Charterhouse of Parma* (Harmondsworth, 1958), pp. 102–3.

64 Hugh Trevor-Roper, *The Invention of Scotland. Myth and History*, ed. Jeremy J. Cater (New Haven, 2008), p. xiii.

65 Peter Fritzsche, *Stranded in the Present. Modern Time and the Melancholy of History* (Cambridge, Mass., 2004), p. 211.

66 Tim Blanning, *The Triumph of Music: Composers, Musicians and their Audiences, 1700 to the Present* (London, 2008), pp. 241–3.

67 Peter Gay, *The Party of Humanity* (London, 1963), p. 273.

68 Paul Langford, *A Polite and Commercial People. England 1727–1783* (Oxford, 1989), p. 96.

69 J.H. Plumb, *The Death of the Past* (London, 1969), p. 129.

70 Edward Gibbon, *The Decline and Fall of the Roman Empire*, pt. 2, ch. 1.

71 See above, p. 34.

72 Hugh Trevor-Roper, 'History and sociology', *Past and Present*, 42 (1968), pp. 15–16.

73 'The French Revolution As It Appeared To Enthusiasts At Its Commencement', composed in 1804 and first published in 1809 in Coleridge's *The Friend* and later as lines 690–728 of Book Ten of *The Prelude* – *The Poetical Works of William Wordsworth*, ed. E. de Selincourt, 5 vols (Oxford, 1940–9), vol. II, pp. 264, 518.

74 Glyndon G. Van Deusen, *Sieyès: his Life and his Nationalism* (New York, 1932), p. 75 n. 3.

75 Edmund Burke, *Reflections on the Revolution in France*, ed. Conor Cruise O'Brien (Harmondsworth, 1968), p. 119.

76 Lord Acton, 'German schools of history', *English Historical Review*, 1, 1 (1886), p. 8.

77 David Blayney Brown, *Romanticism* (London, 2001), p. 198.

78 Thomas Carlyle, 'On History', in George Sampson (ed.), *Nineteenth Century Essays* (Cambridge, 1912), p. 1.

79 Emmanuel Joseph Sieyès, *What is the Third Estate?*, ed. S.E. Finer (London, 1963), p. 117.

80 Quoted in Karl-Georg Faber, *Deutsche Geschichte im 19. Jahrhundert* (Wiesbaden, 1979), p. 57.

81 Jacques Droz, *Le romantisme allemand et l'état. Résistance et collaboration dans l'Allemagne napoléonienne* (Paris, 1966), p. 218.

82 Kenneth Clark, *The Gothic Revival. An Essay in the History of Taste*, with a new introduction and bibliography by J. Mordaunt Crook (London, 1995), p. 72.

83 Robson-Scott, *The Literary Background of the Gothic Revival*, p. 16.

84 Frédéric Hartweg, 'Das Straßburger Münster', in Etienne François and Hagen Schulze (eds), *Deutsche Erinnerungsorte*, 3 vols (Munich, 2001), vol. III, pp. 411–13.

85 Anthony Vidler, 'Gothic revival', in Denis Hollier (ed.), *A New History of French Literature* (Cambridge, Mass., and London, 1989), pp. 610–11.

86 David Cairns, *Berlioz*, vol. I: *The Making of an Artist 1803–32* (London, 1989), pp. 67–8.

87 Michael J. Lewis, *The Gothic Revival* (London, 2002), p. 25.

88 James Macaulay, *The Gothic Revival 1745–1845* (Glasgow, 1975), *passim*.

89 Clark, *The Gothic Revival*, p. 7.

90 Ibid., p. 180.

91 G.W.F. Hegel, *Aesthetics. Lectures on Fine Art*, trans. T.M. Knox, 2 vols (Oxford, 1975), p. 619.

92 Ibid., p. 686.

93 See the commentary by Helmut Börsch-Supan on the painting in the catalogue which accompanied the magnificent exhibition on Schinkel staged at the Victoria and Albert Museum in 1991 – Michael Snodin (ed.), *Karl Friedrich Schinkel – a Universal Man* (London, 1991), p. 104.

94 Georg Forster, *Ansichten vom Niederrhein, von Brabant, Flandern, Holland, England und Frankreich im April, Mai und Juni 1790*, ed. Wilhelm Buchner, 2 vols (Leipzig, 1868), vol. I, p. 24.

95 Ibid., p. 25.

96 It was reprinted as an introduction to his book *Der Dom von Köln und das Münster von Strassburg* (Regensburg, 1842), pp. 1–4.

97 Reprinted in translation in Michael Charlesworth (ed.), *The Gothic Revival 1720–1870. Literary Sources and Documents*, 3 vols (Mountfield, 2002), vol. III, pp. 642–77.

98 Robson-Scott, *The Literary Background of the Gothic Revival*, pp. 131, 159, 213–15.

99 David E. Barclay, *Frederick William IV and the Prussian Monarchy 1848–1861* (Oxford, 1995), p. 31.

100 Robson-Scott, *The Literary Background of the Gothic Revival*, p. 300.

101 For example Thomas Nugent, *The Grand Tour, or a Journey through the Netherlands, Germany, Italy and France*, vol. II (London, 1756), p. 320.

102 William Beckford, *Dreams, Waking Thoughts and Incidents*, ed. Robert J. Gemmett (Stroud, 2006), p. 66.

103 Ibid., p. 68.

104 Gertrude Cepl-Kaufmann and Antje Johanning, *Mythos Rhein. Zur Kulturgeschichte eines Stromes* (Darmstadt, 2003), p. 115.

105 Fiona MacCarthy, *Byron. Life and Legend* (London, 2003), p. 160.

106 Leslie A. Marchand (ed.), *Byron's Letters and Journals*, vol. 5: *1816–1817* (London, 1976), pp. 76, 78.

107 *Childe Harold's Pilgrimage*, Canto 3, stanza 46.

108 Mary Shelley, *History of a Six Weeks' Tour through a part of France, Switzerland, Germany and Holland* (1817) in *The Novels and Selected Works of Mary Shelley*, vol. VIII: *Travel Writing*, ed. Jeanne Moskal (London, 1996), p. 36.

109 Mary Shelley, *Frankenstein, or The Modern Prometheus*, ed. Nora Crook (London, 1996), pp. 119–20.

110 John R. Davis, *The Victorians and Germany* (Oxford, 2007), pp. 62–3.

111 Edward Bulwer Lytton, *The Pilgrims of the Rhine* (London, n.d.), p. 335.

112 Victor Hugo, *The Rhine* (New York, 1845), pp. 105–6. The

first French edition was published in 1842.

113 Ibid., p. 106.

114 Jean-Jacques Rousseau, *The Confessions*, ed. J.M. Cohen (London, 1953), p. 167.

115 Quoted in Andrew Beattie, *The Alps: a Cultural History* (Oxford, 2006), p. 122.

116 Robert Darnton, *The Great Cat Massacre and Other Episodes in French Cultural History* (New York, 1984), p. 242.

117 Edward Chaney, 'The Grand Tour and the evolution of the travel book', in Andrew Wilton and Ilaria Bignamini (eds), *Grand Tour. The Lure of Italy in the Eighteenth Century* (London, 1996), p. 95.

118 William Edward Mead, *The Grand Tour in the Eighteenth Century* (Boston and New York, 1914), p. 104.

119 Christopher Hibbert, *The Grand Tour* (London, 1969), pp. 24–5. I have discussed this in 'The Grand Tour and the reception of neo-classicism in Great Britain in the eighteenth century', in Rainer Babel and Werner Paravicini (eds), *Grand Tour. Adeliges Reisen und europäische Kultur vom 14. bis zum 18. Jahrhundert* (Ostfildern, 2005), pp. 541–54.

120 Quoted in Jean Clay, *Romanticism* (Oxford, 1981), p. 70.

121 Ibid., pp. 74–7.

122 Ibid., p. 73.

123 Ibid.

124 Beattie, *The Alps*, pp. 126, 130.

125 Shelley, *History of a Six Weeks' Tour*, p. 12.

126 James Macpherson, *The Poems of Ossian*, ed. Howard Gaskill (Edinburgh, 1996), p. 5.

127 Macpherson, *The Poems of Ossian*, p. 7.

128 Trevor-Roper, *The Invention of Scotland, p. 103.*

129 Goethe, *The Sufferings of Young Werther*, p. 147.

130 Fiona Stafford, Introduction to Macpherson, *The Poems of Ossian*, p. xv. See also Michael Ferber (ed.), *A Companion to European Romanticism*, pp. 139–40, 184, 243, 315.

131 Fiona J. Stafford, '"Dangerous Success": Ossian, Wordsworth and English romantic literature', in Howard Gaskill (ed.), *Ossian Revisited* (Edinburgh, 1991), p. 50.

132 Ibid., p. 87.

133 Trevor-Roper, *The Invention of Scotland*, p. 118.

134 Ibid., p. 171. Trevor-Roper's conclusions have been given authoritative support by Colin Kidd in 'The Calvinist International', *London Review of Books*, 30, 10 (22 May 2008).

135 See Gaskill (ed.), *Ossian Revisited, passim.*

136 Sassoon, *The Culture of the Europeans*, pp. 81–2; Ilaria Ciseri, *Le Romantisme 1780–1860: la naissance d'une nouvelle sensibilité* (Paris, 2004), p. 55.

137 Edward Dent, *The Rise of Romantic Opera*, ed. Winton Dean (Cambridge, 1976), p. 87; Jean Mongrédien, 'Ossian, ou Les bardes,' in *The New Grove Dictionary of Opera*, edited by Stanley Sadie. *Grove Music Online. Oxford Music Online*, http://www.oxfordmusiconline.com/subscriber/article/grove/music/O004454 (accessed 22 July 2009).

138 Fabienne Moore, 'Early French romanticism', in Ferber (ed.), *A Companion to European Romanticism*, p. 184.

139 Jostein Børtnes, 'The literature of old Russia', in Moser (ed.), *The Cambridge History of Russian Literature*, pp. 16–18.

140 A.H. Sokolov, *Istoriya russkoy literatury XIX veka*, vol. I (Moscow, 1985), p. 50.

141 Derek Sayer, *The Coasts of Bohemia. A Czech History* (Princeton, 1998), p. 53.

142 A.H. Wratislaw, Introduction to *Patriotism, An Ancient Lyrico-Epic Poem*, translated from the original Slavonic (London, 1851), p. 3.

143 Ibid., pp. 7–20.

144 R.J.W. Evans, '"The Manuscripts": the culture and politics of forgery in Central Europe', in Geraint H. Jenkins (ed.), *A Rattleskull Genius: The Many Faces of Iolo Morganwg* (Cardiff, 2005), pp. 51–68. See also Milan Otáhal, 'The manuscript controversy in the Czech national revival', *Cross Currents. A Yearbook of Central European Culture*, 5, 3 (1986), p. 249.

145 Ibid.

146 Andrew Lass, 'Romantic documents and political monuments: the meaning-fulfillment of history in nineteenth century Czech nationalism', *American Ethnologist*, 15, 3 (1986), p. 460.

147 Quoted in Otáhal, 'The manuscript controversy in the Czech national revival', p. 253.

148 Lass, 'Romantic documents and political monuments', p. 460.

149 Quoted in Ibid., p. 254.

150 Václav Holzknecht, *Libuše*, in the booklet accompanying the recording conducted by Zdeněk Košler, Supraphon 11 1276–2 633. See also John Tyrell, *Czech Opera* (Cambridge, 1988), pp. 41–9.

151 Jakob and Wilhelm Grimm, *Deutsche Sagen*, ed. Heinz Rölleke (Frankfurt am Main, 1994), pp. 55–6.

152 Hans-Gert Roloff, 'Der *Arminius* des Ulrich von Hutten', in Rainer Wiegels and Winfried Woesler (eds), *Arminius und die Varusschlacht: Geschichte, Mythos, Literatur* (Paderborn, 1995), p. 214.

153 Robert Ergang, 'National sentiments in Klopstock's odes and *Bardiete*', in *Nationalism and Internationalism. Essays Inscribed to Carlton J.H. Hayes* (New York, 1950); Andreas Dörner, *Politischer Mythos und symbolische Politik. Sinnstiftung durch symbolische Formen am Beispiel des Hermannmythos* (Opladen, 1995), p. 133.

154 Ibid., p. 132.

155 Gesa von Essen, *Hermannsschlachten. Germanen- und Römerbilder in der Literatur des 18. und 19. Jahrhunderts* (Göttingen, 1998), p. 128.

156 Ibid.

157 Caroline Herder, *Erinnerungen aus dem Leben Johann Gottfried von Herder*, ed. J.G. Müller, 2 vols (Tübingen, 1820), vol. I, p. 221.

158 Dörner, *Politischer Mythos*, pp. 156–70.

159 Ibid., p. 175; Werner Hofmann, *Caspar David Friedrich* (London, 2000), pp. 88–93.

160 Ibid., p. 95.

161 Burke, *Popular Culture in Early Modern Europe*, p. 4.

162 Eckart Klessmann, *Die deutsche Romantik* (Cologne, 1981), p. 27. Frederick's comment was made when declining the dedication of a collection of German medieval texts, including *Parzival* and *Tristan* – Horst Steinmetz (ed.), *Friedrich II., König von Preußen und die deutsche Literatur des 18. Jahrhunderts. Texte und Dokumente* (Stuttgart, 1985), p. 340.

163 Klaus Lankheit, 'Nibelungen–Illustrationen der Roman-

tik. Zu Säkularisation christlicher Bildformen im 19. Jahrhundert', in Joachim Heinzle and Anneliese Waldschmidt (eds), *Die Nibelungen. Ein deutscher Wahn, ein deutscher Alptraum. Studien und Dokumente zur Rezeption des Nibelungenstoffs im 19. und 20. Jahrhundert* (Frankfurt am Main, 1991), p. 95.

164 Ibid., p. 28.

165 W.H. Auden, *Forewords and Afterwords*, ed. Edward Mendelson (London, 1973), p. 245. Auden added that Wagner was also 'a very bad hat indeed'.

166 Elizabeth Magee, *Richard Wagner and the Nibelungs* (Oxford, 1990), p. 13.

167 Robert Donington, *Wagner's 'Ring' and its Symbols*, 3rd edn (London, 1974), p. 32.

168 Dieter Borchmeyer, 'Renaissance und Instrumentalisierung des Mythos. Richard Wagner und die Folgen', Saul Friedländer and Jörn Rüsen (eds), *Richard Wagner im Dritten Reich* (Munich, 2000), p. 67.

169 Quoted in Mark Berry, *Treacherous Bonds and Laughing Fire: Politics and Religion in Wagner's Ring* (Aldershot, 2006), p. 21.

170 Ibid., p. 23.

171 *The Poetical Works of William Wordsworth*, eds. E. de Selincourt and Helen Darbishire, vol. 5 (Oxford, 1949): *The Excursion*, Book 6, lines 545–7, p. 203.

172 Quoted in Safranski, *Romantik*, p. 34.

173 Quoted in Hugh Honour, *Romanticism* (London, 1979), p. 218.

174 Michael Levey, *Rococo to Revolution: Major Trends in Eighteenth-Century Painting* (London, 1966), p. 204.

175 Ibid., pp. 32, 235–6.

176 K. Andrews, *The Nazarenes: a Brotherhood of German Painters in Rome* (Oxford, 1964), pp. 20–3.

177 Max Hollein and Christa Steinle (eds), *Religion Macht Kunst: Die Nazarener* (Cologne, 2005), pp. 258–64. This exhibition catalogue contains many excellent colour reproductions.

178 Ibid., p. 130.

179 William Vaughan, *German Romantic Painting* (New Haven, 1980), p. 216.

180 Andrews, *The Nazarenes*, pp. 42–3.

181 Alexander Rauch, 'Klassizismus und Romantik: Europas Malerei zwischen zwei Revolutionen', in Rolf Toman (ed.), *Klassizismus und Romantik. Architekur – Skulptur – Malerei–Zeichnung. 1750–1848* (Cologne, 2000), p. 421.

182 Frank Büttner, 'Cornelius, Peter', *Grove Art Online. Oxford Art Online*, 24 July 2009, http://www.oxfordarton line.com/subscriber/article/grove/art/T019543.

183 H.S. Reiss (ed.), *The Political Thought of the German Romantics* (Oxford, 1955), pp. 145–6.

184 Heinrich von Kleist, *Berliner Abendblätter vom 1ten Oktober 1810 bis zum 30ten März 1811*, facsimile reproduction (Wiesbaden, n.d.), 3, 3 October 1810, pp. 11–15.

185 Klaus Lankheit, *Revolution und Restauration 1785–1855* (Cologne, 1988), p. 68.

186 Barbara Johnson, 'The Lady in the Lake', in Hollier (ed.), *A New History of French Literature*, p. 631.

187 Cranston, *The Romantic Movement*, p. 83.

188 Walter Friedländer, *David to Delacroix* (New York, 1968), p. 94.

189 Honoré de Balzac, *Lost Illusions* (Harmondsworth, 1971), p. 240.

190 Cranston, *The Romantic Movement*, p. 95.

191 F.W.J. Hemmings, *Culture and Society in France 1789–1848* (Leicester, 1987), pp. 173–4.

192 Cranston, *The Romantic Movement*, p. 95.

193 Quoted in Sandy Petrey, 'Romanticism and social vision', in Hollier (ed.), *A New History of French Literature*, p. 661.

194 Quoted in Honour, *Romanticism*, p. 217.

195 George Heard Hamilton, 'Delacroix's Memorial to Byron', *The Burlington Magazine*, vol. 94, no. 594 (September, 1952), pp. 257–61.

196 *Childe Harold's Pilgrimage*, Canto II, stanza 73.

197 'The Isles of Greece', *Don Juan*, Canto III, following stanza 86.

198 Quoted in Peter Cochran, 'Byron's European reception', in Drummond Bone (ed.), *The Cambridge Companion to Byron* (Cambridge, 2004), p. 251.

199 Quoted in Maurice Bowra, *The Romantic Imagination* (Oxford, 1961), p. 149.

200 Ibid.

201 Ibid., p. 153.

202 Ibid., p. 152.

203 William St Clair, *That Greece Might Still Be Free. The Philhellenes in the War of Independence* (Oxford, 1972), p. 19.

204 Jerome McGann, 'Byron, George Gordon Noel, sixth Baron Byron (1788–1824)', *Oxford Dictionary of National Biography*, Oxford University Press, Sept. 2004, online edn, Oct. 2008 [http://www.oxforddnb.com/view/article/4279, accessed 31 March 2009].

205 C.M. Woodhouse, *The Philhellenes* (Cranbury, 1971), pp. 92–3. Jerome McGann has also written 'No English writer except Shakespeare acquired greater fame or exercised more world influence' – 'Byron', as in the previous footnote.

206 Donald H. Reiman and Neil Fraistat (eds), *Shelley's Poetry and Prose*, 2nd edn (New York and London, 2002), p. 316.

207 Frederick Page (ed.), *Byron. Poetical Works* (Oxford, 1970), p. 108.

208 Quoted in P.M.S. Dawson, *The Unacknowledged Legislator. Shelley and Politics* (Oxford, 1980), p. 1.

209 Shelley, *Poetical Works*, ed. Thomas Hutchinson (London, 1904), p. 603.

210 David Kimbell, *Italian Opera* (Cambridge, 1991), p. 392.

211 Piero Garofalo, 'Romantic poetics in an Italian context', in Ferber (ed.), *A Companion to European Romanticism*, p. 250.

212 Roberta J.M. Olson, 'Introduction: in the dawn of Italy', in Roberta J.M. Olson (ed.), *Ottocento: Romanticism and Revolution in Nineteenth-Century Italian Painting* (New York, 1992), p. 14.

213 Fernando Mazzocca, 'Painting in Milan and Venice in the first half of the century', in Ibid., pp. 140–1.

214 David Kimbell, *Verdi in the Age of Italian Romanticism* (Cambridge, 1981), p. 22; John Black, *The Italian romantic Libretto. A Study of Salvadore Cammarano* (Edinburgh, 1984), p. 5.

215 Quoted in John Rosselli, *Music and Musicians in Nineteenth-Century Italy* (London, 1991), pp. 70–1.

216 I have discussed this in greater detail in *The Triumph of*

Music : Composers, Musicians and their Audiences: 1700 to the Present, pp. 264–72.

217 See above, pp. 148–50.

218 James J. Sheehan, *German Liberalism in the Nineteenth Century* (Chicago, 1978), p. 39.

219 Joachim Köhler, *Richard Wagner. The Last of the Titans* (New Haven and London, 2004), pp. 225–30.

220 Stewart Spencer and Barry Millington, *Wagner's Ring of the Nibelung* (London, 1993), p. 281.

221 Ibid., p. 149.

222 William Ashton Ellis, *The Life of Richard Wagner*, vol. IV (London, 1904), p. 442.

223 Martin Gregor-Dellin and Dietrich Mack (eds), *Cosima Wagner's Diaries*, vol. II: *1878–1883* (London, 1980), p. 631. Entry for 25 February 1881.

224 Ibid., pp. 623–4. Entry for 19 April 1873.

225 See above, p. 13. On Wagner and Rousseau, see my 'Richard Wagner and Max Weber', *Wagnerspectrum*, 2 (2005), pp. 93–110.

Conclusion

1 Bryan Gilliam and Charles Youmans, 'Strauss, Richard', in *Grove Music Online. Oxford Music Online*, http://www.oxfordmusiconline.com/subscriber/article/grove/music/40117pg1 (accessed 7 Aug. 2009).

2 See above, p. 102.

3 William Vaughan, *German Romantic Painting* (New Haven, 1980), p. 239.

4 Jethro Bithell, *An Anthology of German Poetry* (London, 1947), p. x.

5   Quoted in Hans-Ulrich Wehler, *Deutsche Gesellschafts-geschichte*, vol. II: *Von der Reformära bis zur industriellen und politischen 'Deutschen Doppelrevolution' 1815–1848/49* (Munich, 1987), p. 207.

6   Quoted in Linda Nochlin, *Realism* (London, 1971), p. 23.

7   Ibid., p. 41.

8   Carl E. Schorske, *Fin de Siècle Vienna. Politics and Culture* (Cambridge, 1981), pp. 24–5.

9   Eugen Weber, *France: Fin de Siècle* (Cambridge, Mass., 1986), p. 147.

10   Schorske, *Fin de Siècle Vienna*, p. 227.

11   Quoted in Ronald Hayman, *Nietzsche: a Critical Life* (London, 1995), p. 163.

12   Quoted in Martin Jay, 'From modernism to post-modernism', in T.C.W. Blanning (ed.), *The Oxford Illustrated History of Modern Europe* (Oxford, 1996), p. 262.

13   Ibid., p. 267.

14   David Watkin and Tilman Mellinghoff, *German Architecture and the Classical Ideal 1740–1840* (London, 1987), p. 178.

15   Nikolaus Pevsner, *An Outline of European Architecture*, 5th edn (Harmondsworth, 1957), p. 285. The first edition was published in 1943.

16   Quoted in Armand Mattelart, *Networking the World, 1794–2000* (Minneapolis and London, 2000), p. 95.

17   Axel Körner, 'Culture', in Mary Fulbrook (ed.), *Europe since 1945* (Oxford, 2001), p. 159.

SUGGESTIONS FOR
FURTHER READING

Texts

Miriam Allott (ed.), *The Poems of John Keats* (London, 1970)

Gerhard von Breuning, *Memories of Beethoven. From the House of the Black-Robed Spaniards*, ed. Maynard Solomon (Cambridge, 1992)

Edmund Burke, *A Philosophical Enquiry into the Origin of our Ideas of the Sublime and the Beautiful*, ed. Adam Phillips (Oxford, 1990)

Edmund Burke, *Reflections on the Revolution in France*, ed. Conor Cruise O'Brien (Harmondsworth, 1968)

David Cairns (ed.), *The Memoirs of Hector Berlioz* (London, 1969)

Michael Charlesworth (ed.), *The Gothic Revival 1720–1870. Literary Sources and Documents*, 3 vols (Mountfield, 2002)

David Charlton (ed.), *E.T.A. Hoffmann's Musical Writings: Kreisleriana, The Poet and the Composer, Music Criticism* (Cambridge, 1989)

S.H. Clark (ed.), *Mark Akenside, James Macpherson, Edward Young: Selected Poetry* (Manchester, 1994)

Samuel Taylor Coleridge, *Collected Letters of Samuel Taylor Coleridge*, ed. Earl Leslie Griggs, vol. I (Oxford, 1956)

Thomas De Quincey, *Confessions of an English Opium Eater*, ed. Alethea Hayter (Oxford, 1971)

Further Reading

Otto Erich Deutsch (ed.), *Schubert. Memoirs by his Friends* (London, 1958)

Lorenz Eitner, *Neoclassicisim and Romanticism 1750–1850*, vol. I: *Enlightenment/Revolution* (London, 1971)

Johann Wolfgang von Goethe, *Faust*, Part One, trans. David Luke (Oxford, 1987), Part Two, trans. David Luke (Oxford, 1994)

Johann Wolfgang von Goethe, *The Sufferings of Young Werther*, trans. Bayard Quincy Morgan (London, 1957)

G.W.F. Hegel, *Aesthetics. Lectures on Fine Art*, trans. T.M. Knox, 2 vols (Oxford, 1975)

H.C. Robbins Landon, *Beethoven. A Documentary Study* (London, 1975)

James Macpherson, *The Poems of Ossian*, ed. Howard Gaskill (Edinburgh, 1996)

H.S. Reiss (ed.), *The Political Thought of the German Romantics* (Oxford, 1955)

H.E. Rollins (ed.), *The Letters of John Keats, 1814–21*, 2 vols (Cambridge, 1958)

Friedrich Wilhelm Joseph von Schelling, *Ideas for a Philosophy of Nature as Introduction to the Study of this Science*, trans. Errol E. Harris and Peter Heath (Cambridge, 1988).

Friedrich Schlegel, *Lucinde and the Fragments*, ed. Peter Virchow (Minneapolis, 1971)

Stendhal, *Life of Rossini*, trans. Richard N. Coe (London, 1956)

Wilhelm Heinrich Wackenroder and Ludwig Tieck, *Herzensergießungen eines kunstliebenden Klosterbruders*, ed. A. Gillies (Oxford, 1966)

Richard Wagner, *My Life* (Cambridge, 1983)

Adrian Williams (ed.), *Franz Liszt. Selected Letters* (Oxford, 1998)

Adrian Williams (ed.), *Portrait of Liszt by Himself and his Contemporaries* (Oxford, 1990)

William Wordsworth, *The Excursion*, E. de Selincourt and Helen Darbishire (eds), *The Poetical Works of William Wordsworth*, vol. 5 (Oxford, 1940–9)

William Wordsworth, *The Prelude. The Four Texts (1798, 1799, 1805, 1850)*, ed. Jonathan Wordsworth (London, 1995)

William Wordsworth and Samuel Taylor Coleridge, *The Lyrical Ballads with a Few Other Poems*, 1798 edn, published *in facsimile* (Woodstock, 1990)

Edward Young, *Conjectures on Original Composition, in a Letter to the Author of Sir Charles Grandison* (London, 1759)

Secondary works

M.H. Abrams, *The Mirror and the Lamp. Romantic Theory and the Critical Tradition* (Oxford, 1971)

K. Andrews, *The Nazarenes: a Brotherhood of German Painters in Rome* (Oxford, 1964)

Joseph-Marc Bailbé, *La Musique en France à l'époque romantique (1830–1870)* (Paris, 1991)

F. M. Barnard, *Herder's Social and Political Thought. From Enlightenment to Nationalism* (Oxford, 1965)

Andrew Beattie, *The Alps: A Cultural History* (Oxford, 2006)

Isaiah Berlin, 'The counter-enlightenment', in *idem, Against the Current: Essays in the History of Ideas* (London, 1979)

Isaiah Berlin, 'Herder and the Enlightenment', in Earl R.

Wasserman (ed.), *Aspects of the Eighteenth Century* (Baltimore and London, 1965)

Mark Berry, *Treacherous Bonds and Laughing Fire: Politics and Religion in Wagner's Ring* (Aldershot, 2006)

T.C.W. Blanning, *The Culture of Power and the Power of Culture. Old Regime Europe, 1660–1789* (Oxford, 2002)

Tim Blanning, *The Triumph of Music: Composers, Musicians and their Audiences, 1700 to the Present* (London, 2008)

Maurice Bowra, *The Romantic Imagination* (Oxford, 1961)

Nicholas Boyle, *Goethe. The Poet and the Age*, vol. 1: *The Poetry of Desire* (Oxford, 1991)

David Blayney Brown, *Romanticism* (London, 2001)

Peter Burke, *Popular Culture in Early Modern Europe* (London, 1978)

Marilyn Butler, *Romantics, Rebels and Reactionaries. English Literature and its Background 1760–1830* (Oxford, 1981)

David Cairns, *Berlioz*, vol. I: *The Making of an Artist, 1803–1832* (London, 1989)

Gertrude Cepl-Kaufmann and Antje Johanning, *Mythos Rhein. Zur Kulturgeschichte eines Stromes* (Darmstadt, 2003)

D.G. Charlton (ed.), *The French Romantics*, 2 vols (Cambridge, 1984)

Ilaria Ciseri, *Le Romantisme 1780–1860: la naissance d'une nouvelle sensibilité* (Paris, 2004)

Kenneth Clark, *The Gothic Revival. An Essay in the History of Taste*, with a new introduction and bibliography by J. Mordaunt Crook (London, 1995)

Kenneth Clark, *The Romantic Rebellion. Romantic versus Classical Art* (London, 1973)

T.J. Clark, *The Absolute Bourgeois: Artists and Politics in France 1848–1851* (London, 1973).

Jean Clay, *Romanticism* (Oxford, 1981)

Maurice Cranston, *The Romantic Movement* (Oxford, 1994)

David Daiches, *Robert Burns* (London, 1966)

S. Foster Damon, *A Blake Dictionary. The Ideas and Symbols of William Blake* (Providence, 1965)

John R. Davis, *The Victorians and Germany* (Oxford, 2007)

Edward Dent, *The Rise of Romantic Opera*, ed. Winton Dean (Cambridge, 1976)

Andreas Dörner, *Politischer Mythos und symbolische Politik. Sinnstiftung durch symbolische Formen am Beispiel des Hermannmythos* (Opladen, 1995)

Jacques Droz, *Le romantisme allemand et l'état. Résistance et collaboration dans l'Allemagne napoléonienne* (Paris, 1966)

David Edmonds and John Eidinow, *Rousseau's Dog: Two Great Thinkers at War in the Age of Enlightenment* (London, 2006)

Herbert von Einem, *Deutsche Malerei des Klassizismus und der Romantik 1760–1840* (Munich, 1978)

Alfred Einstein, *Music in the Romantic Era* (London, 1978)

Lorenz Eitner, *Neoclassicisim and Romanticism, 1750–1850*, vol. I, *Enlightenment/Revolution* (London, 1971)

Reinhold Ergang, *Herder and the Foundations of German Nationalism* (New York, 1931)

Gesa von Essen, *Hermannsschlachten. Germanen- und Römerbilder in der Literatur des 18. und 19. Jahrhunderts* (Göttingen, 1998)

Michael Ferber (ed.), *A Companion to European Romanticism* (Oxford, 2005)

Elliot Forbes (ed.), *Thayer's Life of Beethoven*, revised edn (Princeton, 1969)

Michael Forsyth, *Buildings for Music. The Architect, the Musi-*

cian, and the Listener from the Seventeenth Century to the Present Day (Cambridge, Mass., 1985)

Paul Frankl, *The Gothic. Literary Sources and Interpretations through Eight Centuries* (Princeton, 1960)

Walter Friedlander, *David to Delacroix* (New York, 1968)

Peter Fritzsche, *Stranded in the Present: Modern Time and the Melancholy of History* (Cambridge, Mass., 2004)

Hannelore Gärtner, *Georg Friedrich Kersting* (Leipzig, 1988)

Nigel Glendinning, *Goya and his Critics* (New Haven and London, 1977)

Helmut Grasshoff (ed.), *Geschichte der russischen Literatur von den Anfängen bis 1917*, 2 vols (Berlin, 1986)

F.W.J. Hemmings, *Culture and Society in France 1789–1848* (Leicester, 1987)

Werner Hofmann, *Caspar David Friedrich* (London, 2000)

Werner Hofmann, *Das entzweite Jahrhundert. Kunst zwischen 1750 und 1830* (Munich, 1995)

Richard Holmes, *The Age of Wonder: How the Romantic Generation Discovered the Beauty and Terror of Science* (London, 2008)

Hugh Honour, *Neo-classicism* (Harmondsworth, 1968)

Hugh Honour, *Romanticism* (London, 1979)

Robert Hughes, *Goya* (London, 2003)

Jens Christian Jensen, *Caspar David Friedrich. Leben und Werk*, 10th edn (Cologne, 1995)

James H. Johnson, *Listening in Paris: A Cultural History* (Berkeley and Los Angeles, 1995)

Paul Johnson, *The Birth of the Modern: World Society, 1815–1830* (London, 1991)

Marion Kant (ed.), *The Cambridge Companion to Ballet* (Cambridge, 2008)

Elie Kedourie, *Nationalism*, 4th edn (Oxford, 1993)

E. Kennedy, *A Cultural History of the French Revolution* (1989)

David Kimbell, *Italian Opera* (Cambridge, 1991)

David Kimbell, *Verdi in the Age of Italian Romanticism* (Cambridge, 1981)

John Louis Kind, *Edward Young in Germany* (New York, 1906)

Eckart Klessmann, *Die deutsche Romantik* (Cologne, 1981)

Joachim Köhler, *Richard Wagner: The Last of the Titans* (New Haven and London, 2004)

Klaus Lankheit, *Revolution und Restauration 1785–1855* (Cologne, 1988)

David C. Large and William Weber (eds), *Wagnerism in European Culture and Politics* (Ithaca and London, 1984)

Michael Levey, *Rococo to Revolution: Major Trends in Eighteenth-Century Painting* (London, 1966)

Michael J. Lewis, *The Gothic Revival* (London, 2002)

James Macaulay, *The Gothic Revival, 1745–1845* (Glasgow, 1975)

Fiona MacCarthy, *Byron: Life and Legend* (London, 2003)

Alan Menhennet, *The Romantic Movement* (London, 1981) [on Germany]

Timothy Mitchell, *Art and Science in German Landscape Painting, 1770–1840* (Oxford, 1993)

Jean Mongrédien, *La Musique en France des Lumières au Romantisme 1789–1830* (Paris, 1986)

Charles A. Moser (ed.), *The Cambridge History of Russian Literature* (Cambridge, 1989)

Martin Myrone, *Henry Fuseli* (London, 2001)

Rudolf Neuhäuser, *Towards the Romantic Age: Essays on Pre-romantic and Sentimental Literature in Russia* (The Hague, 1974)

Thomas Nipperdey, 'In Search of Identity: Romantic Nationalism', in J.C. Eade (ed.), *Romantic Nationalism in Europe* (Canberra, 1983)

Thomas Nipperdey, *The Rise of the Arts in Modern Society* (London, 1990)

Linda Nochlin, *Realism* (London, 1971)

Roberta J.M. Olson (ed.), *Ottocento: Romanticism and Revolution in Nineteenth-Century Italian Painting* (New York, 1992)

Roy Pascal, *The German Sturm und Drang* (Manchester, 1953)

Alfonso E. Pérez Sánchez and Eleanor A. Sayre (eds), *Goya and the Spirit of Enlightenment* (Boston, 1989)

Giorgio Pestelli, *The Age of Mozart and Beethoven* (Cambridge, 1984)

Nikolaus Pevsner, *Academies of Art – Past and Present* (Cambridge, 1940)

R. Porter and M. Teich (eds), *Romanticism in National Context* (Cambridge, 1988)

T.J. Reed, *Schiller* (Oxford, 1991)

Alexander Ringer (ed.), *The Early Romantic Era. Between Revolutions: 1789 and 1848* (London, 1990) [on music]

W.D. Robson-Scott, *The Literary Background of the Gothic Revival in Germany* (Oxford, 1965)

Charles Rosen, *The Romantic Generation* (New York, 1996)

Robert Rosenblum, *The Romantic Child from Runge to Sendak* (London, 1998)

Robert Rosenblum and H.W. Janson, *Art of the Nineteenth*

Century. Painting and Sculpture (London, 1984)

Stephen Rumph, *Beethoven after Napoleon. Political Romanticism in the Late Works* (Berkeley, Los Angeles and London, 2004)

Rüdiger Safranski, *Romantik. Eine deutsche Affäre* (Munich, 2007)

Jim Samson (ed.), *The Late Romantic Era. From the Mid-Nineteenth Century to the First World War* (London, 1991) [on music]

Donald Sassoon, *The Culture of the Europeans from 1800 to the Present* (London, 2006)

Derek Sayer, *The Coasts of Bohemia: A Czech History* (Princeton, 1998)

H.G. Schenk, *The Mind of the European Romantics* (Oxford, 1979)

Hans-Joachim Schoeps, *Deutsche Geistesgeschichte der Neuzeit*, vol. 3, *Von der Aufklärung zur Romantik* (Mainz, 1978)

James J. Sheehan, *German History, 1770–1866* (Oxford, 1989)

James J. Sheehan, *Museums in the German Art World. From the End of the Old Regime to the Rise of Modernism* (New York, 2000)

Stewart Spencer and Barry Millington, *Wagner's Ring of the Nibelung* (London, 1993)

William St Clair, *That Greece Might Still Be Free. The Philhellenes in the War of Independence* (Oxford, 1972)

G.L. Strachey, *Landmarks of French Literature* (London, n.d.)

Rolf Toman (ed.), *Klassizismus und Romantik. Architektur – Skulptur – Malerei – Zeichnung 1750–1848* (Cologne, 2000)

Hugh Trevor-Roper, *The Invention of Scotland: Myth and History*, ed. Jeremy J. Cater (New Haven, 2008)

Raymond Trousson, 'Jean-Jacques Rousseau et son œuvre dans la presse périodique allemande de 1750 à 1800', *Dix-huitième Siècle*, 1 (1969)

John Tyrell, *Czech Opera* (Cambridge, 1988)

William Vaughan, *German Romantic Painting* (New Haven, 1980)

Alan Walker, *Franz Liszt: The Virtuoso Years, 1811–1847*, revised edn (London, 1989)

John Warrack, *Carl Maria von Weber*, 2nd edn (Cambridge, 1976)

L.A. Willoughby, 'Classic and romantic: a re-examination', *German Life and Letters*, 6 (1952)

C.M. Woodhouse, *The Philhellenes* (Cranbury, 1971)

INDEX

Index